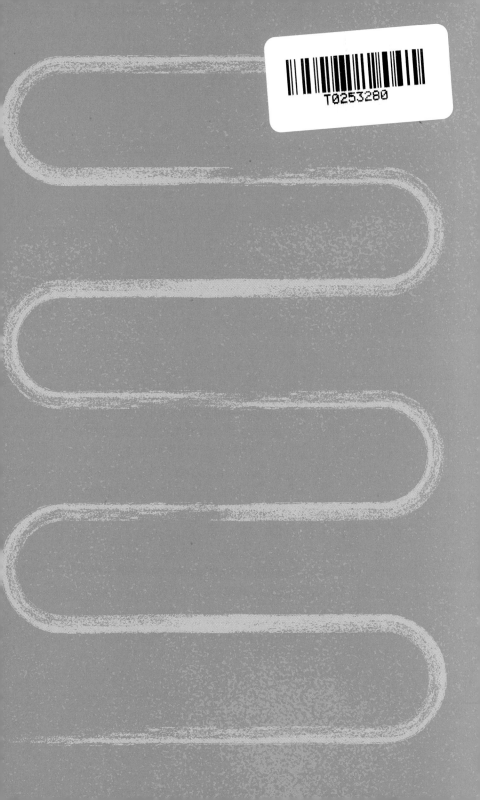

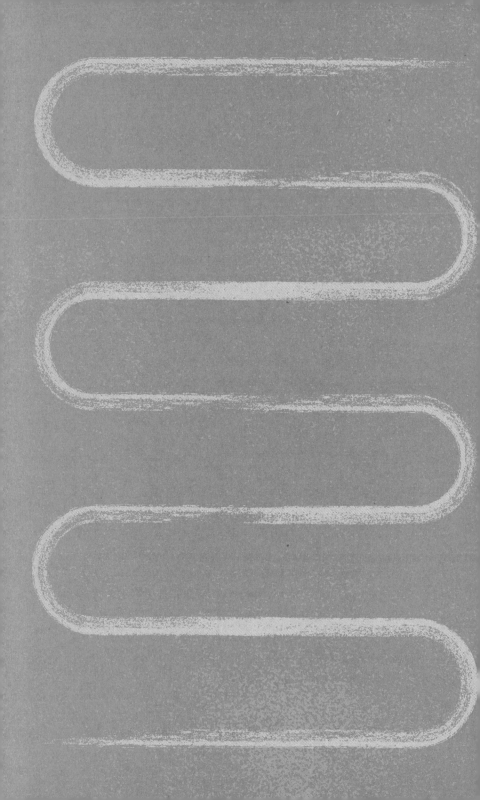

PRAISE FOR

THE ENNEAGRAM FOR TEENS

"In *The Enneagram for Teens,* Ainsley Britain has distilled the Enneagram's wisdom into a relatable and engaging guide tailored for teenagers. This book is a transformative compass for the younger generation, offering them valuable insights and a head start in their lifelong journey of understanding themselves and others. I know this book will positively impact the lives of teenagers, parents, and educators alike."

Amy Wicks, *The Simply Wholehearted Podcast*
host, author, and Wholehearted coach

"What a resource! Ainsley has a knack for taking confusing subjects and breaking them down into easy-to-digest nuggets of wisdom, always pointing us to Christ. From comparing the layers of our personality to a cake (I love her for this) to using characters to help illustrate each Enneagram number, this book is so light yet so transformative! As a mom of teen girls, I am so thankful for every word Ainsley writes. She makes you feel like you are sitting together on her back porch sipping tea, but your conversation 'accidentally' changes your life in the process. Her knowledge of the Enneagram and her love for Jesus are married together so well. She uses the tools of personality evaluation to help you understand how you were created and how to use those gifts to grow, heal, and thrive!"

Katie Bulmer, *Truth for your Twenties* podcast host, author, and mentor

"This book is a game changer for those navigating the exciting yet complex journey of being a teenager. Ainsley's writing is engaging and relatable, making the Enneagram easy to grasp, but she dives deeper by addressing important life topics often missing in other Enneagram guides, such as faith and career choices. Ainsley's infectious personality shines through her words as she shares vibrant illustrations and compelling stories, making the Enneagram come to life in a fun and meaningful way. Because Ainsley is a trusted authority in this space and has already influenced countless teens through her writing and speaking, this book is a must-read for anyone seeking to discover themselves during this pivotal life stage."

Tyler Zach, author of the 40-Day Enneagram Devotional series

"A roadmap to propel you beyond self-discovery toward spiritual growth during the teen years, where the struggle to understand yourself and others and make sense of your faith feels visceral at times. Ainsley is a wise mentor and kind friend in the pages of this book—one I wish I had as a teen."

Meredith Boggs, author of *The Journey Home: A Biblical Guide to Using the Enneagram to Deepen Your Faith and Relationships*

"As a mom of teenage girls, I am desperate for resources to help me better communicate with my daughters and give them language we can all use and understand to navigate these challenging years. The Enneagram is a tool both the church and corporate America have used to help build communication skills and conflict resolution among its staff, and it can also be a gift to parents looking to do the same in our homes. Ainsely does a beautiful job of using real-life, applicable situations to help teens discover not only their strengths, but their weaknesses, inviting them to look more deeply into how God made them as they learn how to develop healthy relationships, navigate their emotions, and set goals for their future. It's a beautiful thing that as humans we aren't all packaged the same, and this book is a sweet gift to help teens see beyond the wrapping and into the deepest parts of their heart desperate for love, purpose, and understanding."

Natalie Runion, bestselling author of *Raised to Stay*

THE ENNEAGRAM FOR TEENS

A **COMPLETE GUIDE** to **SELF-DISCOVERY** and **SPIRITUAL GROWTH**

AINSLEY BRITAIN

 ZONDERVAN

ZONDERVAN

The Enneagram for Teens
Copyright © 2024 by Ainsley Britain

Published in Grand Rapids, Michigan, by Zondervan. Zondervan is a registered trademark of The Zondervan Corporation, L.L.C., a wholly owned subsidiary of HarperCollins Christian Publishing, Inc.

Requests for information should be addressed to customercare@harpercollins.com.

Zondervan titles may be purchased in bulk for educational, business, fundraising, or sales promotional use. For information, please email SpecialMarkets@Zondervan.com.

ISBN 978-0-310-15523-2 (softcover)
ISBN 978-0-310-15540-9 (audio)
ISBN 978-0-310-15537-9 (ePub)

Library of Congress Cataloging-in-Publication Data

Names: Britain, Ainsley, author.
Title: The enneagram for teens : a complete guide to self-discovery and spiritual growth / Ainsley Britain.
Description: Grand Rapids, Michigan : Zondervan, [2024] | Includes bibliographical references. | Audience: Ages 13 and up | Summary: "From author and enneagram coach Ainsley Britain comes a comprehensive introduction to the enneagram personality test, specially crafted for teens and young adults. In The Enneagram for Teens, readers will discover their type and gain valuable insights into their relationships, faith, future selves, and more. As one of the most popular personality frameworks, the enneagram has been helping people gain a deeper understanding of themselves and others for decades. In The Enneagram for Teens, Ainsley Britain distills her vast knowledge of the enneagram into an approachable, easy-to-use guide that's perfect for beginners. Filled with insights and tips on navigating stress, relationships, faith, friendships, and more, The Enneagram for Teens is an invaluable tool for finding your path and becoming the best version of yourself"— Provided by publisher.
Identifiers: LCCN 2023026399 (print) | LCCN 2023026400 (ebook) | ISBN 9780310155232 (paperback) | ISBN 9780310155379 (ebook) Subjects: LCSH: Enneagram. | Teenagers— Psychological testing. | Typology (Psychology) | BISAC: YOUNG ADULT NONFICTION / Inspirational & Personal Growth | YOUNG ADULT NONFICTION / Religious / Christian / Inspirational
Classification: LCC BF698.35.E54 B758 2024 (print) | LCC BF698.35.E54 (ebook) | DDC 155.2/60835—dc23/eng/20240226
LC record available at https://lccn.loc.gov/2023026399
LC ebook record available at https://lccn.loc.gov/2023026400

Published in association with The Bindery Agency, www.TheBinderyAgency.com.

Cover Design: Micah Kandros/Micah Kandros Design
Interior Design: Denise Froehlich

Printed in the United States of America

24 25 26 27 28 LBC 5 4 3 2 1

CONTENTS

AUTHOR'S NOTE

My Enneagram journey began when I was twenty-two years old. Over a vanilla latte salted with my tears, a friend handed me a book with a weird word on it I had never seen before.

"Here, you might like this. I think it'll help you work through some things during the grieving process," she said.

I had just been through a brutal breakup, and the statement that prompted her gift was, "I just don't understand him, how he left, or why I even stayed so long in a relationship I knew wasn't good for me."

I had no idea the information bound in that book would change my life.

I curled up in my bed that evening, turned off the TV playing whatever romantic comedy I had been crying to, and cracked open a book with the word *Enneagram* written in a large font across the front.

"How do you even pronounce that word?" I thought.

(In case you've wondered the same thing, here you go: **eh-nee-uh-gram**.)

I was already fascinated by sociology and why humans are

the way we are. So when I read a book that revealed so much about myself and the personalities of my friends and family, I was hooked! You couldn't pry that book from my post-breakup, chocolate-covered fingers for at least a month.

The Enneagram didn't just tell me about the behaviors, strengths, and weaknesses of myself and those around me. It really focused on the "why" behind our actions, emotions, and motivations. In fact, that's how I personally describe it: a personality assessment that explains the "why" behind your thoughts, behaviors, and actions.

As I went through the steps of grief from the breakup, I suddenly started understanding some of the miscommunication between my ex and me when we argued, why we would get so frustrated when the other person did something a certain way, and, ultimately, why it didn't work out. That book gave me the closure I wanted so badly but wouldn't ever get from him. Truthfully, it was the only closure I ended up needing, because it was more than closure. It was a true understanding of the thought processes and emotions behind our actions, especially mine!

Those realizations gave me my confidence back and allowed me to heal faster. I was able to love again, starting with the person in the mirror. That book wasn't my only source of healing, of course, but it was a huge part of the puzzle. Reading its pages, coupled with counseling and tapping into my faith, was what helped me get through. Then I carried what I learned through the Enneagram into other areas of my life.

I understood my family members better, along with my friends, peers at school, and even some teachers! I also learned more about myself than ever before. In the past, I'd taken the Myers-Briggs Type Indicator, DiSC, StrengthsFinder, Love Languages, and honestly any other personality assessment

I'd ever heard of. I loved them all and still believe each one is helpful, but the Enneagram was different. I felt so seen and understood on paper that it freaked me out! It was like the thoughts I believed only I had were written right in front of me. Not only that, but apparently there were other people who had those same thoughts and were just like me?!

The Enneagram was more than a list of what I was good at or gifted in. It was a description of my heartbeat: how I feel loved, how I get hurt, why I do the things I do and feel the way I feel at any given moment. It told me facts about myself that I didn't even know and showed me how to use some weaker parts of my personality as strengths.

It was so enlightening in my world then, and continues to be today as I learn more with every coaching session, casual conversation, or new book that comes out. I believe it can do the same for you—teaching you more about yourself than you ever knew and bringing a comfort to any fears and self-doubts you're wrestling with. The wrestling may continue, of course, but throughout the pages to come, together we will walk along the path to the healthiest version of ourselves. The most coffee-stained, dog-eared, worn-on-every-edge books on my bookshelf are about the Enneagram, and I hope this book becomes that on your shelf!

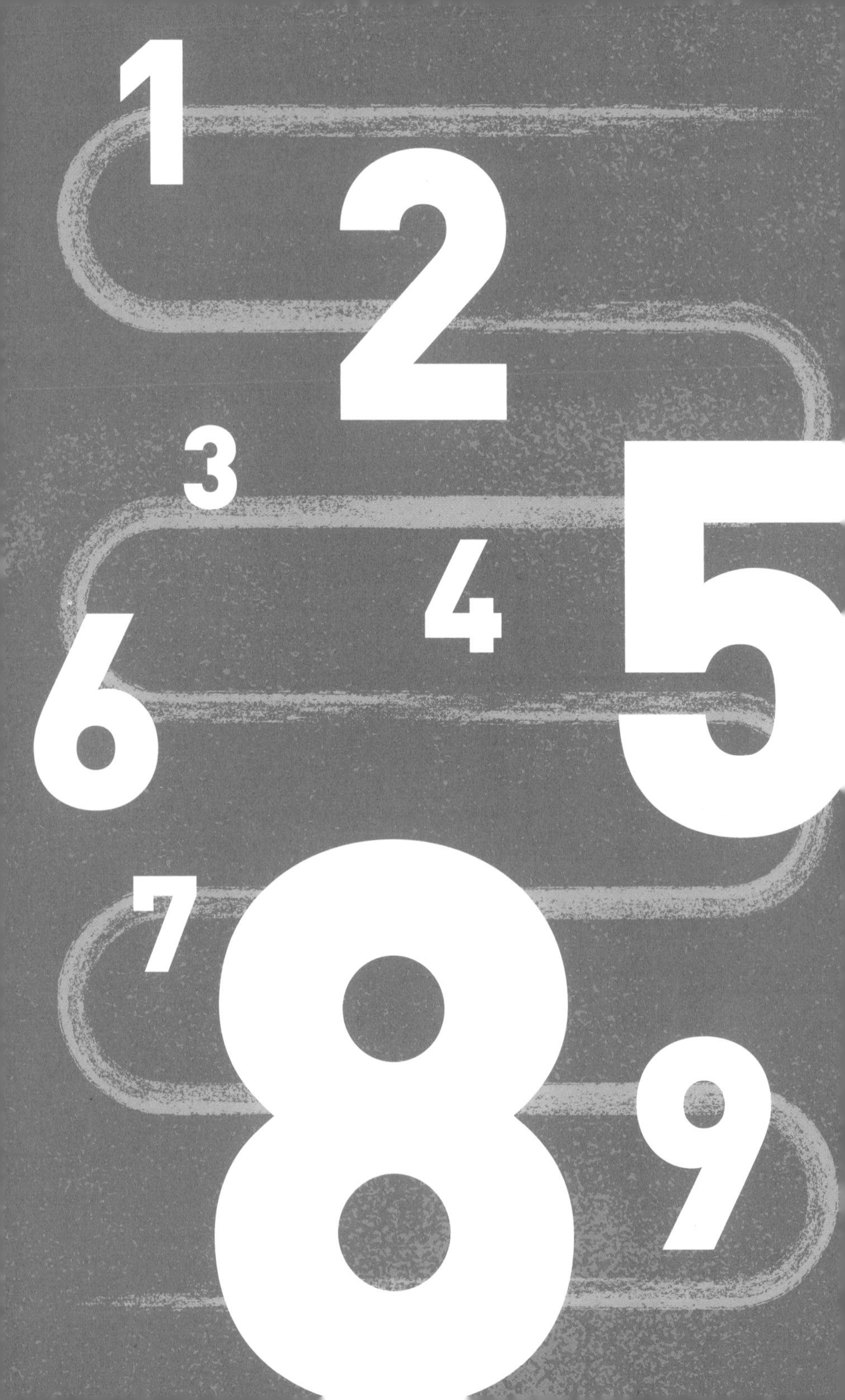
1
2
3
4
5
6
7
8
9

INTRODUCTION

What Is the Enneagram?

O kay, okay, enough about my personal introduction to the Enneagram. Are you wondering, "What IS the Enneagram already?" Or have you already taken assessments, reflected, and feel like you know your type? Whatever the case may be, I hope you're filled with new insights as we dive into the various complexities of the Enneagram.

I am a certified Enneagram coach through the Your Enneagram Coach Program by Jeff and Beth McCord. I cannot speak more highly of how they approach the Enneagram and all that it encompasses. I love how they define the Enneagram when they say, "The Enneagram is a tool, like a GPS, to help you know where you are, where you are heading (whether on your best path or veering off course), and how to get to your healthiest destination."[1]

While their definition is simple, it helps show how much the Enneagram encompasses. The more you unpack the Enneagram, the more complex it seems. But let's start with the basics. When you break down the word *Enneagram* into two parts, the "ennea" is Greek for *nine* and represents the nine types on the "gram," or diagram. This is what it looks like:

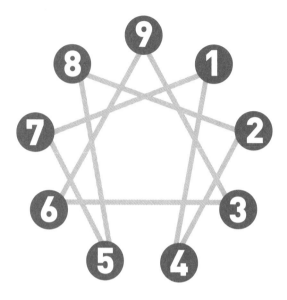

In the chapters to come, we will do a deep dive into each type, but for now I'd love to do a brief overview of each number type that you see above, based on their core fear and core desire—their core motivators—which is ultimately what determines your Enneagram type.

TYPE ONE: The Moral Compass

The ethical, principled, and perfectionistic type fears being corrupt or a bad person, while their core desire is to have integrity, be balanced, and be a good person. They're always looking for "true north" when it comes to being morally and ethically sound.

TYPE TWO: The Helper

The warm, generous, people-pleasing type is the Helper. They fear being unwanted or unworthy of being loved, so their core desire makes a lot of sense: they wish to be wanted or loved.

TYPE THREE: The Heroic Leader

The productive, image-conscious, success-oriented type has the core fear of being worthless or experiencing failure, while their core desire and biggest motivation is to feel valuable or worthwhile.

TYPE FOUR: The Unique Creative

The romantic, creative, and expressive type fears they have no identity or significance in the world. The opposite is true for their core desire, which is to have an identity and be known for something.

TYPE FIVE: The Deep Thinker

The analytical, private, innovative type is motivated by their desire to be competent and capable. They fear being useless or helpless.

TYPE SIX: The Loyalist

The witty, suspicious, and responsible type fears being without safety or security. Their core desire is feeling safe and secure in every area of life, whether that is in relationships, at work, or in their physical environment.

TYPE SEVEN: The Adventurer

The spontaneous, busy, and fun type desires to be content and satisfied. Their core fear is being in pain emotionally or being deprived.

TYPE EIGHT: The Challenger

The confident, intense, and dominating type fears losing their power or feeling controlled by their circumstances, environment, or people around them. On the flip side, their core desire is to protect themselves and the ones they love.

TYPE NINE: The Gentle Peacemaker

The agreeable, complacent, laid-back type fears loss or being separated from those they love, whether that is physically or emotionally. Their core desire is to have inner stability and peace of mind.

As you read these, you may feel like more than one applies to you. That is totally normal! You'll likely see little glimpses of your personality in a few different types, but we are hoping to eventually veer toward your main type. The more we get into each type and the behaviors that accompany them in various scenarios, the more you may feel drawn to a certain type as "yours."

As we dig into the specifics of each type, including levels of health, wings (related types), and so on, you'll see how much variety lies within each type, and how two people who may both be an Adventurer (type Seven) can still seem quite different! So as you explore the Enneagram, keep in mind that you and someone else could have the same type while still being quite unique from each other. It's really fun to see how people with the same type are similar and different, because as people, we are more than just a personality type.

Now, before we go any further, it's important to know something: the Enneagram, this book, and any others on the topic are merely tools. They're not the end-all-be-all, not the Bible, and not the answers to all of life's problems. We'll chat more about this, but I wanted to make sure you knew that while my magnetic attraction to the Enneagram was instantaneous, it did not replace what I believed when it came to my faith.

Faith's Role in Your Enneagram Journey

One of my favorite Enneagram thought leaders and authors is Ian Morgan Cron. He says this about the Enneagram: "The Enneagram doesn't put you in a box. It shows you the box you're already in and how to get out of it."[2] Yes, yes, yes! We tend to walk through life with a mindset of "That's just who I am," accepting the lies and limitations that discourage us from walking in our full potential. When you are able to see the limitations you have been living with and how you can shake them off and move forward with a heightened sense of self and your strengths, you're able to see yourself how God created you. As we talk about types and numbers, I want to remind you, you are more than that.

You are a complex, beautiful, wonderful creation of God, and the most important thing you can take away from our time together is that he created you on purpose, just the way you are. Now, does our free will give us some bumps and bruises along the way in life? Sure, but thankfully he is also called the Great Physician, and when we partner with him, we see transformation and healing.

The Enneagram changed my life because it helped me understand why God made me the way he did. When I took a deeper look at myself, I stopped picking apart things I would change and I started to think, "Whoa, I'm actually beginning to feel 'fearfully and wonderfully made' by my Creator, like Psalm 139 says. I get it. I get it, and I appreciate it. I'm thankful for the traits he's given me, and honestly, now I don't feel so alone."

My transformation happened not because of the Enneagram on its own, but because it drew me closer to my Heavenly Father. It allowed me to partner with him on a mission and use the gifts and talents I now understood to better the lives of others and heal the wounds that had scabbed over in my heart. In the same way, the Enneagram is a helpful tool that can change your life, but transformation only happens when you ask God about the things you learn about yourself. Ask your Creator about his creation!

The Enneagram can feel like an intense process of learning so much about your inner world, but I pray it will give you a deep appreciation for who God made you to be. Look, this journey is going to be deep, light, hard, easy, fun, painful—really, all of the things. I hope you enjoy your time in the chapters to come and read them ALL, not just your type! Yeah, caught you. (I bet you tried to skip this introduction altogether, you little Enneagram Seven, you. I love you already.) I love every single type so much, y'all! And you will too, if you take the time to read and understand them.

It's likely you know someone who falls into each of these types, and this book will help you build stronger relationships with those people and understand them on a deeper level. It can improve your friendships, romantic relationships, family dynamics, and your relationship with your Creator.

Let's Break It Down

When I was in high school, I remember a teacher saying that math builds on itself. You lay a foundation, then the next lesson you learn is built on that foundation. Then there's another layer, and another. Well, it's not that fun to compare the Enneagram to math, and while onions have layers, I love sprinkles, so the picture we're going with is a cake! We'll assemble each layer of the cake as we discover more about the Enneagram, remembering that it builds on itself, and we will also return to the foundation if it gets confusing at any point.

The first layer is what we've covered in this introduction: an understanding of the basic structure, the principles of the Enneagram, and a brief description of each type. As we dive more into each specific type, we will cover core motivations, levels of health, stress and growth paths, and wings. And if you're ready to dig even deeper into the Enneagram, we'll address triads, tritypes, and subtypes in chapter 10.

I've used the term "core motivator" a couple of times, so allow me to paint a picture. What do I mean by core motivators? Let's say you and I are invited to a birthday party. We get gifts for the friend we are celebrating, and when we walk in, we discover we brought the same gift! What are the odds?

When we think about core motivators, instead of focusing on the behavior of simply bringing the same gift, the Enneagram focuses on *why* you brought that gift and *why* I brought that gift. That's because an Enneagram Two would've brought that specific gift for one reason, and an Enneagram Six could've brought it for an entirely different reason.

For example, if the gift were a new bag, the Two may have given it to their friend because they remembered it's their favorite color, while the Six may have given it to that person because it's a great way to stay prepared and have everything you need in one place! We see the same behavior, and both are thinking of ways they can bless that person, but there are different motivations behind it. That is why this layer is so close to the base of our cake. It really gets to the core of your motivations and personality, instead of just observing behaviors and pointing out strengths and weaknesses.

Below is a glossary of terms you will read about a lot in this book. Feel free to come back and reference this list as needed.

The Enneagram: According to Beth and Jeff McCord, it's a tool or a GPS to help you know where you are, where you're heading, and how to get to your healthiest destination. It truly helps us understand the "why" behind some of our thoughts and behaviors so we can become more self-aware and create more harmonious relationships with ourselves, God, and others.

Core Motivators: Your core desires and core fears drive the decisions you make and the emotions you feel. The root of these core motivators has to do with messages you received as a child. Whether the messages were perceived or directly communicated, they stuck with you and are the source of the core motivators. We will get into the specifics in the coming chapters.

Wounding Childhood Messages: One piece of the puzzle that contributes to the full picture of each type is the wounding childhood message we received. Whether actual or perceived, these messages helped shape our Enneagram type, cement our core motivations, and influence how we view the world. Despite the way the name sounds, these are messages related to typical childhood experiences, not specifically traumatic ones. If you've experienced a traumatic event, the best place to process that is with a professional counselor or therapist.

As you read the messages, you may think all of them are relevant to everyone. It's true that you may relate to a few of the fears across types, but pay attention to which one you think you fear the *most* for a clue about your Enneagram type. Then consider where that message may have come from.

Healthy vs. Unhealthy: There are ranges of behaviors for each type that cover how someone may act when they're confident in their identity in Christ, a little less confident, or a bit lost or confused. For example, a mentally healthy Three behaves differently from an average Three, who behaves differently from an unhealthy Three. Typically, it's most common to live your day-to-day life at your average level of health, but we are hopefully always self-improving to be as healthy mentally and emotionally as possible!

Stress and Growth Paths: When someone is experiencing a moment or season of stress, they show unhealthy behaviors of another type. In a moment or season of growth, they will show healthy behaviors of a different type. This is typically caused by a specific event and only lasts for a short amount of time.

Wings: These are the types on the right and left of your main type. They are NOT the next two types you score on an assessment. For instance, if you are a One, your wings are Nine and Two. Each type pulls behaviors from the types on either side of it and can portray a lot of them or just a few. You may have one dominant wing, use them equally, or barely use them at all. It's totally up to you how much or how little you utilize your wings. There is usually a natural inclination toward one wing, but you can definitely choose how you use each. The McCords call them the "salt and pepper" of your personality, which I love because it paints a fun picture of exactly how they bring some seasoning to who you are!

Journey: A cheesy word I can't help but use when it comes to the Enneagram and your experience with it.

Okay, you have the foundation laid and are about to enjoy the layers of this personality cake!

Are you ready to dive in, friend? Grab a fork and let's get started!

Using the Enneagram

Imagine we are on a hiking trail. We have a backpack full of snacks, supplies, and anything we could need to have a safe and successful trek. We look around and appreciate God's creation and everything he made for us to enjoy.

Now, think of the Enneagram as your backpack full of helpful insights that allow you to see yourself as God's wonderful creation. Your journey along life's path will have fewer injuries and heartaches because you are a little more prepared than you would be without your backpack. When a friend joins you on the trail, you'll know how to best walk with them. If a family member joins you, the same will be true. You'll feel equipped for the expedition ahead, and when something unexpected happens, you'll understand your reaction or response better.

Not only is the Enneagram helpful in navigating our own "why" behind the things we do and how we feel, it's also helpful when it comes to understanding our relationships, faith, even what we may want out of a future career. We will dive into more on each of these things with every type in the upcoming chapters.

Keep in mind as we go, the Enneagram is not a game of MASH that dictates your future; it is a tool that can help you navigate some things using self-reflection and empathy. For me, the Enneagram dramatically improved my communication with family, friends, strangers, etc. It taught me the importance of speaking to each person's preferred communication style so we can have effective conflict resolution. In that process, I learned there is no *right* way to communicate, just a peaceful way, which is doing our best to understand where the other person is coming from.

When you discover your type or the types of those around you, there's something extremely important to note. A couple of guidelines, if you will. It should never be used to shame or blame anyone, including yourself. I feel like I should say that again. It should *never* be used to shame or blame *anyone, including yourself.* What do I mean by that? Because we will discover some of the deepest heart longings and motivators behind the types, it's easy to blame some behaviors on simply being that type. For example: "I have to unload the dishwasher you just loaded because I'm a One and I like things done a certain way." In reality, this isn't a behavior that should be explained away or ignored. Instead, you should take time to understand why you feel compelled to redo what has already been done and work to establish a healthier mindset (psst, your type can help you do that!).

It's also easy to shame others for some stereotypical behaviors of their type, and that's not okay either. For example: "You're such an Eight. You just can't keep your opinion to yourself." First of all, rude. Second of all, even if making their thoughts known is a common behavior for that type, that doesn't mean it's okay to make someone feel bad about it. When I was studying the McCords' approach, I loved how they talked about the Enneagram not being a shield to hide behind or a sword to cut people down with.[3] It's important to keep this principle in mind as you work through the Enneagram.

The other rule or guideline when it comes to sharing this tool with the people around you is that it's important not to "type" other people. Meaning, when you're talking about the Enneagram with someone who doesn't know much about it yet, do not assign them a type based on the behaviors you observe.

For example: "You love reading and you're an introvert, so you must be a Five!" You can make an educated guess for yourself, and they *may be that type,* but projecting your assumptions onto them can be confusing. The best way you can support them in their journey is by allowing them to discover what type they believe feels most true for themselves.

When meeting someone and understanding their Enneagram type, treat them with empathy. They may be a different type than you, and they might not be at their optimum level of mental and emotional health. As we noted above when talking about the health aspect, most people are going through life at an average level of health. As nice as it would be, we can't all be operating in the fullness of our worth and value all the time, so speak life over everyone you meet, noting their strengths and gifts. The culture we live in today tends to "cancel" people they don't agree with, but if we truly all agreed on every detail and acted exactly the same, what kind of world would we be living in?

One thing my counselor told me that radically shaped how I view those around me is this: "People are doing the best they can with the tools they have." It's true, isn't it? Some people don't have as many tools as others, and they can only operate with the ones they have. If you're trying to go on a hike and you have a map but no shoes, you will have a difficult time. You'll know what direction you're heading in, but you'll be stepping on sharp objects the whole time!

As you discover the Enneagram types of those around you, always remember people are doing the best they can with the tools they have. As an Enneagram coach, my job is to put more tools in your hands so you are best equipped for your journey ahead. Backpack? Check! Map? Check! Shoes? Check!

Another key thing to remember is that while your personality can change as you age, your core motivators do not. Since the

Enneagram is based on motivators, your type doesn't change. But your type does take a while to develop, which is why I don't necessarily recommend settling into your type until you're closer to the middle of your college years or so. But the self-discovery process can be so rewarding that it's never too soon to start exploring! And what you start to learn now about types and where you might fit can help you better understand yourself now, as well as where you may be headed.

If you're under the age of twenty-one, give yourself time and grace as you research the types to see which feels the truest. Treat it like it's a marathon rather than a sprint. Put on a type like you would a pair of glasses, trying it on through seasons and situations in life, then try on another type and see how that fits. Most of all, enjoy your journey toward self-discovery!

Finding Your Enneagram Type

So, how do you find your type? The best way to discover your Enneagram type is by researching each one and deciding which feels the truest. As you read this book and learn more about discovering your type, it will be tempting to base your decision off the behaviors described in the chapters. However, it's more about the *why* behind the behavior than the behaviors themselves, so be sure to pay close attention to the fears and desires of each type. Also pay attention to how you feel when reading about each type. Yours is likely the type that makes you the most uncomfortable as you read, or makes you think, "How is this reading my mind?"

While this is definitely the most effective route, it is the most labor-intensive. If that feels overwhelming, another option is to take an assessment and research the top three types it gives you. Your type could very well be in those top three! If you're interested in taking an assessment, you can find my favorite at enneagramwithab.com/enneagramresources. If you still don't feel like you've discovered your type, contact a coach to help you through the process. (Ahem, I've heard the author of this book may be a decent coach and can be contacted at the above website.)

Regardless of the route you take, be patient and take your time in the process. The self-discovery journey can be a wild ride, and it's more important to be accurate than to arrive quickly.

A few tips as you go through the discovery process:

1. Be gentle with yourself. Try not to beat yourself up about the parts of you that you don't like or wish were different. We are all a work in progress!
2. The Enneagram often feels like it focuses on the negative aspects of our personality, but like Suzanne Stabile says, "We don't know ourselves by what we get right; we know ourselves by what we get wrong."[4] This is so true and helps us identify our type quicker than if we were focusing solely on the positive. If you feel like the negative is starting to weigh on you, refer back to Tip #1.
3. As you discover more about yourself, I pray you find a sense of wonder about how God created you and develop a deeper relationship with him. The Enneagram is a helpful tool, but keep top of mind that true transformation comes through a relationship with God.

By the time you finish this book, I imagine you'll think, "Okay, I know my main type, but now I feel like I'm just a combination of every type." Because it's true! We really are all of the types in various degrees. When you consider your main type, stress and growth paths, wings, and so on and so forth, you're covering almost all nine types right away! And we are humans, so, naturally, we are more peppered with personality than any book or online assessment lays out.

My hope is you'll understand more about the Enneagram, grow in empathy for those around you, and appreciate who God made you to be. I pray you will fiercely love the person looking back at you in the mirror so you can show up in the world with a wild confidence you've never known before. May you feel seen and equipped with everything you need to show up for yourself and those around you in the healthiest way possible.

Whew—it's going to be a lot of information and a lot of fun along the way. Lace up those hiking shoes, my friend! We are about to head straight to the type One trailhead and learn all about the nine different types.

Quick! Pop Quiz!

1. What is the Enneagram?

2. Is it one of many helpful tools or the only one we should ever use?

   _____

3. Fill in the blanks: The Enneagram should never be used to _____ or _____ anyone.

4. The Enneagram is helpful information, but where is real transformation found?

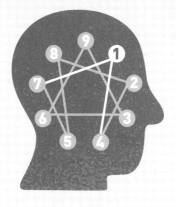

CHAPTER 1

Type One:
THE MORAL COMPASS

You Might Be a One If . . .

1. You immediately notice when something is wrong or could be improved.
2. You want every situation to be fair for everyone.
3. Details are important to you.
4. You need to know the rules; then you determine if you agree with them or not.
5. You're disappointed if people don't pull their weight.
6. You try to be unbiased when problem-solving, separating your emotions from the issue at hand.
7. As a child, you had a lot of responsibility placed on you.
8. It's difficult for you to let go and not have resentment.
9. You've been told you are critical or judgmental.
10. You have a harsh inner critic, always telling you that you should and could be better.

Examples of an Enneagram One

Jill was in a group project for school. The assignment was to create a news station with branding, a location, and a niche, and then decide what segments they would include in each of the shows. There were various other types in the group and one clear leader of the pack. While Jill wasn't the leader, she did keep notes for the group when they met, and she always knew the guidelines for the project. She was organized and on time for every meeting.

When the leader of the group assigned tasks, Jill noticed two of her classmates had very few tasks, which also required little time and attention, while the rest of the group had lengthier to-do lists. She spoke up about the imbalance and suggested the tasks be reshuffled so they were fairer.

The leader rolled their eyes and pushed back on Jill's objection. Jill pushed harder, insisting the roles be balanced. Eventually, her suggestions led to change within the group, and everyone had the same amount of work.

Jill left the meeting with the impression it was successful, and while the two classmates who originally had fewer items were not her biggest fans, the rest of the group was relieved and thankful she shared her thoughts. She created a balance within the group that made it run smoothly and allowed everyone to participate equally.

Max loathed when his dad came to his baseball games. It's not that they had a bad relationship—they were best friends and did almost everything together, including playing video games, running whatever errands were needed, and working on the old motorcycle. But Max dreaded the car ride home after his baseball games. His dad always had something to correct, a way Max could improve. A suggestion here and there was okay, but noting something after every single game felt excessive, and Max's patience grew thin. That's because Max was already thinking about things he should've done better, so having someone else point out ways he should improve felt overwhelming and like he had failed.

One night, after winning the state championship, they got into the truck to head home. Max hopped in, buzzing with excitement and thinking there was no way his dad could have something to critique this time. He felt like he had played perfectly, which he believed was the standard. His dad started the truck and said, "You've got to work on holding your bat higher. I tell you every time."

That comment pushed Max over his edge. He yelled, "Dad, come on! We *won state*, and you still have something to say about what I did wrong? Back off!"

His dad was stunned. "Whoa, bud, I had no idea you were this frustrated with me. I'm only trying to help."

From that point on, his dad offered congratulations and encouragement before any suggestions, which Max appreciated. And Max vowed to speak up when he felt criticized so they could both be aware and solve the problem quickly.

What Makes Up a Type One

Type Ones are known as the Reformer, the Perfectionist, and the Idealist. They are our moral compass friends who genuinely want to be a good person. They would never steal, cheat, or do something that would make them appear immoral. They're the type that cannot tell a lie and are usually right in an argument because they've gathered all the facts. (Since they want to make sure they *are* right!)

Typically, Ones are organized and always want to improve things, but these traits can cause them to fall into crippling perfectionism and criticism. Ones have an inner critic that tends to be harsher and louder than those of other types. My mom is an Enneagram One and says, "There's always a better way for everything." She's in her head all of the time, thinking of ways things can be enhanced or run smoother—even when they seem to work fine already.

Ones are extremely good at problem-solving and can jump into that mode very quickly, which makes them great in a crisis. They enjoy the challenge of problem-solving and like helping others, so it's a win-win! Unless, of course, they hop into that mode when the person talking just wants to express their emotions and feel heard without getting a list of solutions. They may offer advice when it's not asked for or get offended when someone doesn't follow their suggestions. This is a tough hurdle to overcome, but the more growth the One achieves, the more they are able to hold advice loosely and know that it's still helpful, even if the person doesn't "obey."

Their **core fear** is being corrupt or a bad person. They strive to not only be seen as perfect but *be* perfect. I previously mentored a girl who would beat herself up and hold herself to unrealistic standards, and much of the work we did focused on giving herself grace and not letting the inner critic win. This is incredibly challenging for type Ones, which is why they can often be plagued by fear and self-doubt. The **wounding childhood messages** Ones believe are "It's not okay to make mistakes" or "You have to be perfect." Both their core fear and core desire stem from this belief.

A phrase we hear often in childhood is, "Practice makes perfect." This can actually be harmful for Ones, because it implies perfection is possible. Since Ones are especially inclined to strive for perfection, this can lead them to burn out as they fail to set boundaries around their practice. As they continue to try to feed the monster of perfectionism, it turns into their inner critic, which can stay with them into adulthood. This is also an example of how a statement that's meant to be motivating can be perceived as a wounding critique.

Their **core desire** is to have integrity, be balanced, and be a good person. In order to do that, they may have rigid disciplines and be hard on themselves. Routine is often their best friend; it gives them a plan and a purpose to pursue. Therefore, veering from their routine can cause some anxiety. They desperately want to be morally sound, which is why they are the moral compass friend we can always count on to do what is right. Their desire for things to be fair is why people look to them for guidance and honesty.

The Different Levels of a Type One

A **mentally and emotionally healthy One** is an incredible advocate for change, inspiring those around them and creating strategies to complete their vision. Their wisdom is magnetic, and they inspire others to seek the truth.

They feel responsible for creating maturity and fairness around them, which they do well. They are able to silence their inner critic, and they understand how to approach someone or something gently and lovingly. A healthy One is free from the need to control themselves and others, which allows them to let go of resentment or anger.

If you feel you could be a One, the most effective way to move toward health is partnering with the Lord to let go of what needs to be released, then opening your hands to what he wants to place in them. Some other things you can do are:

1. Take time for yourself and do the things you love so you can relax and let the small things go. Engage in a hobby or try something new and exciting that feels relaxing.
2. Work on living unoffended. This is one of the most radical life changes a One can make, and it is absolutely possible. Living unoffended means you lay expectations down, focusing more on gratitude and grace. You let go of feeling entitled to people's time, attention, space, or affection, and instead accept it as a gift.
3. Get in touch with your inner critic and silence it. The best way to do this is through therapy or counseling. Both provide a safe space to lay out your worries and feelings and identify any triggers that may make the critic's voice louder. When you're able to identify which "shortcomings" are the most triggering, you can move past them and forgive yourself, which spills over into the relationships around you.
4. Try breathing exercises when things feel overwhelming. My favorite one is called "box breathing." Draw an imaginary box in the air, starting with one line up as you inhale for four seconds, then hold your breath as you move your finger to the right for four seconds, exhale as you move your finger down for four seconds, and lastly, hold your breath for the last four seconds. Repeat this until you start to feel more at ease.
5. Work on accepting nuance, gray areas, or things that seem to be "flaws." Find the beauty in each of these things and know that everything will be okay; it doesn't have to be perfect. (Did your inner critic just say, "Yes, it does"?)

The **average One** is typically more judgmental or reactive, especially if they feel like they can improve or change the person or situation at hand. Their inner critic is loud, and it is harder to tune it out. What ends up happening is a cycle of trying to please the inner critic by working tirelessly to be perfect, but since the critic can never be satisfied, the cycle continues and leaves the One feeling hopeless and frustrated. In the midst of striving for perfection, they may become self-righteous and think very highly of themselves when compared to others. They may also have a thought that sounds like, "If I can't be perfect at something, I'll at least be better than everyone else."

The average One is usually a rule follower, unless they don't agree with the rule. When that happens, they will try to change the rule or ignore it entirely because they feel like they have a better idea of what the "right" way would be (not because they're trying to be rebellious).

The **unhealthy One** can be harsh with those around them, and explosive and cruel with their words. The inner critic is so loud, it's debilitating and spills out onto those around them, alienating people and causing them to not want the One present. Unhealthy Ones are blinded by their mistakes, which makes them feel like they're in sinking sand. When they're making a decision, sometimes the thought "Everyone is wrong except for me" can creep in. This is a red flag that they're in an unhealthy place.

If you feel like you're in this place, please don't let anger win. Practice some of the healthy One habits so you'll be able to move toward a place of peace and growth.

When under stress, type One shows the unhealthy behaviors of type Four in how they behave and how they feel. That means they might withdraw from friends and family so they can work through their emotions by themselves or feel frustrated that the people around them are misunderstanding their need to make things fair and right.

Their thoughts also start to feel confusing as emotion rises up to silence logic. You may see the once calm and collected One start to panic, which can send them into a spiral of despair. Sometimes the pressure they feel they are under is too much, and their reaction is a desire to be free from responsibility and the weight the inner critic puts on them.

Ones can hold a lot on their shoulders, but when it gets too heavy, it seems like they begin to crumble from the weight of it all. Though people may not see it, because shame tells Ones they have to hide their emotion so they appear strong all of the time.

When in growth, type One shows the healthy behaviors of type Seven in how they behave and how they feel. Color fills their cheeks again as they come alive with enthusiasm and joy. They have a new appreciation for the world and finally feel free! They can take a breath and find the awe and wonder they may have buried inside themselves. This is such a relief to see in a type One!

Finally able to relax, they pour out grace and see that many people are doing their best with the tools they have, and as a result the One discovers the criticism that often plays as a reel in their mind isn't always helpful to share out loud. As Ones grow, they may also become more accepting of their own flaws and mistakes and more compassionate toward themselves. This can involve a willingness to forgive themselves and to let go of perfectionistic standards. It's a beautiful sight to see a type One let their guard down and enjoy the things they love most!

Their **wings** are type Nine and type Two—the Peacemaker and the Helper. Remember, wings are the numbers on either side of your main type and add a little flavor to your personality! You can have one primary wing or use them both equally.

When leaning toward their type Nine wing, Ones seek to understand the world and advocate for justice through teaching or sharing information. They may be more willing to compromise and find middle ground, rather than insisting on their own way. Tapping into the peacemaking wing means they may also be more open to other perspectives and less rigid in their thinking.

Clarity and focus are priorities for Ones in this mindset, as well as maintaining harmony in their relationships and environment. Both the Nine and the One tend to struggle with anger, however, so it's important to pay attention when that starts bubbling to the surface.

When leaning into their Two wing, Ones are aware of the needs of the people around them and are able to improve their community. This type and wing combination is usually more people-oriented; they feel empathy easily and give the best advice! They have a heart for serving their community while problem-solving in an approachable way. Boundaries may be tricky for them, though, as they tend to overextend themselves to support other people. They can even end up being a bit controlling, so that's something to pay attention to.

Getting Along with a Type One

Honesty and directness are valued by Ones when it comes to **conflict resolution**. They will debate back and forth with you if they believe they are right, ensuring all angles of the situation have been settled before moving on, so be prepared to defend your side and talk things through. Ones appreciate structure and clarity, so when trying to resolve conflict, make sure you are clear with them about how you feel and that you're recalling the facts to the best of your ability. If you can make your case, the One will listen to your perspective and (perhaps begrudgingly) admit you are correct.

When it comes to communication, Ones have a sense of pride in their work and skills, so a compliment about something they did correctly or well will help soften any criticism. In order to believe they are a good person, they really want to hear, "You are good," from those around them. Whether you're telling them you appreciate their work ethic or their guidance, that phrase will go a long way. But they usually know when you're being fake, so if it's not sincere, don't say it.

If you're resolving conflict with a One, it helps to let them communicate first so they feel heard and then approach the conversation with a problem-solving mindset. If you're discussing something that could be taken personally, make sure you take a nonjudgmental route so they don't close themselves off to you.

An example of a healthy confrontation they will be more receptive to might go like this:

Hey, I really appreciate when you did ____ and made ____ impact. It showed that you want to do the right thing, and I appreciate that. Can we talk more about ____? I'd like to share my thoughts with you so we can problem-solve together.

Choosing a Career as a Type One

When it comes to choosing a vocation if you're a type One, think about roles in society that enact change and make a difference in the world. Law enforcement officers, judges, philanthropists, or social workers are examples of career paths that may be perfect for an Enneagram One who enjoys social justice and making a difference in the world.

Ones typically have a strong work ethic and are unafraid of challenges, which means they often end up in leadership roles. Depending on how the One is using their wings, they may even prefer to be the second-in-command so they can be productive and have fewer people to manage or less conflict to mediate. Accuracy, problem-solving, making things right, and helping others are also huge motivators for type Ones. You may also see this strength play out in a role like teaching and human resources!

While a One could do well in any role, they may be less inclined to love a job that requires them to be ungenuine, such as a job in sales or advertising. Entertainment could also be a field an Enneagram One may not enjoy, as it often is nonlinear and unpredictable, unable to satisfy their need for routine and stability.

The careers listed above are not comprehensive by any means. Any type could truly have any career. At the end of the day, as long as the work environment motivates the One and allows them the opportunity to create positive change, they will thrive!

Type Ones and Faith

As far as the Enneagram One and their relationship with faith, it can definitely look different based on their level of health. An important thing for a One to remember is that no matter what, they can trust the Lord over their inner critic to guide them. He loves his children, and their actions cannot reduce his love for them. If you are a One, please read this closely: Your actions cannot reduce God's love for you.

As rule followers, Ones can often beat themselves up if they don't live up to their standard of perfection. This is a tough mindset to change, but it's crucial to remember that the Lord is not expecting perfection, just presence. You do not have to be perfect, friend. His mercies are new every morning (Lamentations 3:22–24). Sit with him in his presence, and you will begin to feel a shift of faith. The harsh ideas you once believed will soften, and you will be able to rest in God's provision and care. He welcomes us into his presence and allows us to shed the idea of perfection so his strength can be made perfect in our weakness (2 Corinthians 12:9–10).

Type Ones in Love

How does a One show up in a romantic relationship? Perfect, of course! Okay, kidding, but they are usually very loyal and honest due to their desire to be a "good" person. They typically look for a partner who has similar values and boundaries, and someone who can balance their personality. While they are usually the ones who are all buttoned-up, they appreciate someone with a carefree attitude. Just not so carefree that they throw all caution to the wind.

While Ones appreciate someone who is different than them, those differences can also be challenging and uncomfortable. They may struggle with their romantic interest's new ideas or habits if they don't align with what they are already used to. The good news is this tension of sorts creates engaging conversation because it gives each person an opportunity to consider differing opinions and experience how someone else views the world.

As we looked at in their conflict resolution style, a One will work tirelessly to prove they are right. But once you can come to a place where you both feel heard and agree, the process can build the relationship and help you both better handle disagreements in the future.

As you spend more time together, you might find them confessing things you think are trivial and silly, but even small things can really weigh them down until they express them. Make sure you don't say the things they are sharing are silly, because when they express what has been heavy to them, it means they trust you! This is extremely honorable of them, as it can lead to quick conflict resolution and it's an amazing trait to have in a partner.

And if you are a One in a relationship, make sure you don't view the other person as an improvement project. Take time to see the beauty in their unique traits and gifts. Likely, those traits are what attracted you to that person in the first place. Be open to their ideas, plans, ways of doing things, and feedback, as uncomfortable as that sounds. This will help keep you from focusing on what you would change about your partner, which can be exhausting for the relationship. This will also challenge you to open your mind to a list of endless possibilities and stay flexible.

Ultimately, the more you're able to let your guard down and allow someone to love you completely, the more you will be able to relax and settle into the relationship. The more you lower your guard, the more you can appreciate the person for who they are and the traits they bring to the relationship, instead of seeing things you'd change about them or the relationship in general.

If you are in a relationship with a One, bring the positives to light when they feel stressed or overwhelmed so you don't add to their stress. Highlight the good in what they are doing to help silence their inner critic. Also, keep in mind that their inner critic can be so intense, they might take it out on you, sounding harsh and critical about things you do. Remember they don't mean to be so intense, and give them grace when you're able.

Type Ones with Family and Friends

Often, our family members (read: those closest to us) are the ones who see the worst of us. Whoa, that sounds severe, but it's true. Because we have known them the longest and the deepest, they've been witness to a side of us no one else ever sees or understands. Let's call this side the shadow side. Not only do family and friends see the worst of us, they may see aspects of who we really are deep down, or who we want to be. The truth is, the reason these people see the hidden side of us is because we feel the most comfortable with them. We believe they aren't going anywhere or that their love is unconditional. And while it's good to have that security, it's important to protect our relationships with these people and pay attention when we are behaving in unhealthy ways toward them.

Those closest to a type One may see their "sillier side"—like when a One breaks a rule if they feel like they won't get caught! Close family and friends may also notice a One searching for distractions from their inner critic, including unhealthy outlets to deal with the amount of pressure that falls on their shoulders.

While Ones are usually very outward focused, they may finally feel free to be more inwardly focused or "greedy" around those they love. They also may be more demanding about what they need and how they expect those needs to be fulfilled. Ones should be careful to self-correct and adjust course if they see themselves falling into these patterns.

If you have someone in your life who is a One, here is how you can love and support them well:

1. Give them the grace they won't give themselves. They are usually very hard on themselves, so show them that a mistake or misstep will not cost your relationship.
2. Remind them of the good impact they are making on your life. They want to make a positive difference, so let them know they are and what that means to you.
3. Make a difference together. Join them on their mission to make the world a better place by serving or volunteering

somewhere with them. You can take this opportunity to see the world through their eyes and values.

4. Speaking of doing something together, type Ones really appreciate when people follow through on their plans. Do your best not to miss what you have scheduled. Life happens, of course, and that's okay. But be sure to communicate as early as possible if you have to change plans.

5. Letting an Enneagram One vent or process without interrupting is a great way to love them too. When they are sitting still and mentally walking through a situation, listen without giving advice unless they ask for it.

Advice for Your Type

I have a little trick for you if you are an Enneagram One struggling with your inner critic. Often, the inner critic is the loudest when it comes to status or a role at work (which for you right now likely includes school). Whether the inner critic is in your ear during exams or at your part-time job, it's important to not let it win. So I recommend you name your inner critic. I don't care what you name it, but I think the more ridiculous the name, the better. The goal is to be able to recognize the inner critic and not take it seriously.

For an example, let's call it Biscuits. Biscuits has given you a hard time every day of your life, and you know their voice so well that it sometimes haunts you in your sleep. The next time you hear Biscuits, tell yourself, "Ugh, there goes Biscuits again, trying to cripple me into believing I can and should be better." The more you identify the critic's instruction or voice, the more you can ignore it and move on with your day.

15

A Letter to an Enneagram One

Dear One,

I know it's harsh, the inner critic. I know it just wants to help, but what's helpful about pointing out the imperfections you work so hard to avoid? I hear your heart when you desperately strive to do what's right and fair. You are the true north of truth, and we need you.

You are good. You are okay. You are wonderful, balanced, and, yes, usually right. I pray you work on giving yourself grace and not letting the inner critic win. Name it and silence it. It will not win. If you feel like there is a lot on your shoulders, here is your permission slip to lay it down, hand it over. Perfection is a lie, and your best is good enough, I promise.

The world is better just because you're here. Thank you, dear One.

Are you a type One? Before we move on to the next type, there's one thing I want you to know. When the Lord sees you, he sees your heart. He knows you long to be good and righteous, and he loves you unconditionally. As soon as you ask for it, you are forgiven. Walk in confidence, dear One, that God made no mistakes when he made you.

Have you learned something new in this chapter? In the lines below, write down what you don't want to forget about this type and answer the following reflection questions:

In what ways do you embody type One? Are your habits more of a healthy One or an unhealthy One?

_____

_____

In what ways do you differ from type One?

_____

_____

Do you know anyone who seems to fit type One? How might you encourage them toward healthy One habits?

_____

_____

What's something you can take from this chapter and apply to your life?

_____

_____

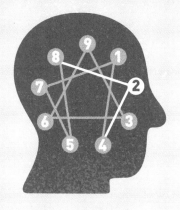

CHAPTER 2

Type Two:
THE HELPER

You Might Be a Two If . . .

1. You enjoy making people feel seen and heard through meaningful conversation.
2. You care what people think of you.
3. You are drawn to powerful or influential people.
4. When someone needs something, you find it nearly impossible to say no.
5. You love being asked for advice, but if you're tired or burnt out, it begins to feel draining.
6. You often feel like other people don't help as much or as well as you do.
7. You usually know what people need or want as if you can read their mind, and you're disappointed when people can't do the same for you.
8. You are sensitive to criticism.

9. You never want to seem needy or selfish.
10. You tend to overcommit.

Examples of an Enneagram Two

Lauren sighed a breath of relief as she sat down to meet with her counselor, Melissa. She finally felt free to say what was on her mind.

"I just don't have amazing two-way friendships," Lauren cried. "It seems like I'm always the one reaching out, and they never do."

Melissa guided her through the emotion, then asked, "Have you told them how you feel?"

"Well, no," Lauren said. "I don't want them to think they hurt my feelings."

Melissa replied, "But have they?"

Lauren looked down, crossed her legs, and admitted, "Yeah, they have."

Melissa validated her feelings and then took it a step further. "When your feelings are hurt, what do you wish they would do?"

Lauren thought for a minute and said, "I wish they would text me."

"And how will they know they hurt your feelings and need to text you if you don't tell them you were hurt?"

The realization washed over Lauren's face. She was so worried about everyone's feelings that she invalidated and quieted her own, leading to resentment and feeling misunderstood. After the session, she texted a friend and asked if they could meet for coffee so she could share what was weighing on her heart.

Conner dropped everything and hopped into the car with Caroline when she asked him to ride with her to get gas because it was dark and she was nervous to go alone. He got out, pumped the gas for her, and was happy to do so. A man in need approached them at the pump and asked for money. Conner wasn't carrying any cash, so he asked if he could get the man something to eat and drink inside. He walked with this man inside, let him pick out what he wanted, and wished him well.

Caroline sat in the car in awe of Conner's actions. She was amazed by him but also felt guilty that she'd asked him on this venture and he ended up pumping gas and spending money, things she wasn't sure he was thrilled to do on a random Thursday night. When he got back in the car, she apologized for the inconvenience. Conner, being an Enneagram Two, was confused by her apology.

"Are you kidding?" he said. "It's an honor to be able to bless him tonight. I'm so thankful you asked me to join you! It made my night to help both of you out."

What Makes Up a Type Two?

Type Twos are known as the Helper, the Caregiver, or the Supportive Advisor. They are the friend who will drop everything to help you move even though their schedule is packed, the one who has broad shoulders to cry on, the one who is ready to fill whatever role you need from them. Twos have a unique ability to be in a conversation with someone and just know what they need to hear in that moment. They tend to be very nurturing and supportive, and they often put the needs of others before their own.

On the outside, they appear selfless, but there may be an ulterior motive under the surface. Twos like to feel needed and helpful, so their apparent selflessness can in fact be for their own benefit (whether they're totally conscious of it or not). If you are a Two, you may have the hardest time learning about your type because it shines a light on some characteristics you'd rather not face. For example, the fact that pride is a huge struggle for the Two. When less healthy, they begin to think they are indispensable, a quality that defines their self-worth. Because of this, they can feel slighted when their help isn't acknowledged, and they may also struggle with codependency.

Their **core fear** is being unwanted or unworthy of being loved. To make sure they are loved and valued, they may try to force themselves into people's lives and become indispensable, instead of doing the work to believe they are loved just because they exist. A Two usually believes they are worthy of love, but not too much love. It's a confusing place to be. Their internal narrative might sound like, "Yes, I'd love to get dinner and hang, but if you offer to help me do something I really need help with, I will feel indebted to you because I wasn't able to prove *why* I'm worthy of love if you're the one helping me." I'm exhausted just thinking about it.

The **wounding childhood message** that correlates with this fear is "You can't have your own needs/desires" or "It's important to always please others." Whether real or perceived, the little Two starts to believe their needs don't matter, so they eventually stop voicing them. This carries into adulthood, and not only does the adult Two feel like their needs don't matter, they think they are a burden to anyone else. Their catchphrase may be, "No worries if not!" when asking for a favor. When, in fact, there are a lot of worries if they feel like they have inconvenienced someone else.

Their **core desire** is the opposite—to be wanted or loved.

Typically, everything they do is from this motivation. Are they bringing a birthday gift? Helping you study for a test? Whatever it is, know this is their heart posture. They are seeking that validation, typically going above and beyond to get it.

Twos can get into a cycle of needing to be needed, which causes them to overextend themselves and get too involved in the lives of those around them. Eventually, this will create burnout, and they will start to feel taken advantage of. Twos want to love people well, and they usually do! But paying attention to the motivation behind the helping is important.

Before we go further, if you're a Two (or anyone who likes showing their love through actions), there's something I want you to remember as you read this chapter: If you find yourself helping for the "wrong" reasons at times or feeling frustrated that people don't appreciate what you do, that doesn't mean you're a bad person—you just have a coping mechanism that isn't always healthy for you. You're still loved even when you don't run yourself ragged to prove it!

The Different Levels of a Type Two

The **healthy Two** is not only self-aware of their own emotions and needs, but able to communicate them clearly to those around them. More importantly, they're able to communicate them without shame or doubt. They can verbalize what is on their heart without fear of rejection or abandonment because they know that their true identity lies with the Lord, who will never reject or abandon them.

The beauty of the healthy Two is that they can give freely of their time, attention, and resources without expecting anything in return. They can love unconditionally with humility and confidence.

If you think you sound like a Two, a few ways to become a healthy version include:

1. Address your own needs. Really take the time to think through what they are, how can they be met, and what expectations are attached to them. When you can see them, you can address them more carefully and clearly. Then spend time with yourself, doing something you love for you. It should be something that will fill *your* cup so your love can come from an overflow instead of a desperation.

2. Find someone you can talk to, like a therapist, counselor, or mentor. This will give you a relationship where you don't have to worry about being "enough," as it's their role to support you. This is a great way to verbally process your needs as well.

3. Pay attention to your motives when you help someone. How does it make you feel? (Be honest!) Are there strings attached to the helping? Work on cutting those strings and giving freely and quietly. When you do something that honors or helps another person, don't harp on it or bring it up over and over.

4. Remember that not everyone will like you, and that's okay. This can be such a hard pill to swallow, but their reaction to you is often more a reflection of that person's perspective than you as a person. However, you can still use that opportunity to look inward and see if there's something that needs some fine-tuning in you. For example, could the person tell you were seeking affirmation or being insincere? And while it's fine to see if there's something you can learn, don't obsess over it.

5. Work on establishing and maintaining healthy

boundaries with those around you. Consider a person in your life and ask yourself: How far am I willing to let them in and give access to my heart, resources, and energy? Your answer will likely vary for each person, honestly—your best friend gets far more access than the person you see every day just because you have a class together. I often think of the Target logo when I think of boundaries. Who do I have on the outer circle and who is on the inner circle? The boundary exists in between. As giving as Twos are, giving too much of themselves can be harmful in the long run, so maintaining that distance makes a big difference.

The **average Two** turns on the flattery or charm quickly when they feel like they need validation or want attention. They are usually the ones highly focused on their friend who needs the most love and affection, in the hope it will be reciprocated when they themselves need it. They can become possessive and needy, exactly what they try to avoid. If this neediness goes on for a while, they will become a martyr, sacrificing themselves for people who didn't necessarily ask that of them in the first place, which leaves the Two feeling taken advantage of, even though they might have had ulterior motives from the beginning.

The **unhealthy Two** can be manipulative and harmful, using their words to make people feel guilty or small. They do things to get sympathy from others and can be a hypochondriac to see who will help them. Exhausted from overextending themselves, they get frustrated and feel taken advantage of if anyone asks for any help, a favor, or even advice.

They end up wearing themselves out trying to be indispensable to those around them and are out of touch with their own motives. This leads them to believe they are kind and selfless, which in turn leads to pride and arrogance. This mindset can cause them to feel entitlement, resentment, and rage when people aren't grateful for their actions, and they end up blaming others for their suffering so they don't have to take accountability.

When under stress, a type Two shows the unhealthy attributes of a type Eight in how they behave and how they feel. This means they may become explosive and volatile, extremely pointed with their words, and manipulative to get what they want. (If you're a Two reading this, this is probably when you want to close the book, but I promise it's worth it to keep reading.) And since a time of stress usually means the Two is also at their unhealthy level, their desire to blame others for their problems may even lead them to isolate themselves from the person "at fault" so they feel what it's like to not have the Two's undying love and support anymore. Two, as soon as you start to feel these things happening, it's your cue to self-care. Journal, draw a bath, go on a walk, anything that helps you recenter.

When in a season of growth, a type Two shows the healthy attributes of a type Four in how they behave and how they feel. Self-awareness becomes their superpower, and they can clearly evaluate their true motives toward a person or a situation. They finally take care of their own needs and even vocalize them to the people closest to them. They're able to walk away from their shame, knowing that even with the traits they don't love about themselves, others still love them. Finally understanding it's okay to have feelings like anger and sadness, they accept those emotions and are able to bring them before the Lord so he can purify their hearts. True, unselfish wisdom shines through. They also may feel more creative than before, picking up a new hobby just for fun and just for themselves.

The **wings** for type Two are One and Three—the Moral

Compass and the Heroic Leader. Remember, wings are on either side of your main type and add a little flavor to your personality! When a Two is leaning toward the One wing, you may see a more reserved personality who is focused on fairness and social justice. They're able to recognize the needs of those around them and serve people intentionally. They may be self-critical at times, however, causing some insecurity to rise up. When they develop the feeling they're not good enough on their own, they're also more likely to isolate themselves so they aren't a burden to anyone else in their life. They want others to need them, but they don't want to be seen as needy.

A type Two with a Three wing is typically more outgoing and often is someone who loves hosting gatherings or parties that build connection with others in a warm environment. They may have everyone over for a game night or bring the best snacks to the library to study for a test. Because they are very good at reading people, they're extremely relational and seek acceptance. They're more concerned with being liked and are typically great communicators full of optimism and passion. They may struggle with being image-conscious and people-pleasing in an effort to make sure others like them. If they feel like someone doesn't like them for any reason, they may do whatever it takes to change that person's mind.

Getting Along with a Type Two

When communicating with a Two, it's very important that you help them feel heard and encourage them to express themselves and their needs. The reason for this is that they often feel unheard because they don't share what's on their heart enough, choosing to stay silent in fear others will not want them or will leave if they admit they need help. And as they keep those needs inside, they grow more and more upset by the minute. This reaction isn't on you, though. They also need to learn to be vocal with their needs and understand it's okay to express them with the people they trust. So how can you best help them and keep your relationship healthy when things need to be discussed?

Conflict resolution can be tricky when communicating with a type Two. They are typically conflict avoidant, so I definitely advise treading lightly. The most effective way to communicate any critical feedback to a Two is via a compliment sandwich.

Start with something positive or affirming, then go in with the feedback, and close with another positive or affirming statement. If you're an Enneagram Eight (who are often straightforward and direct), you may be rolling your eyes at the type Two needing this kind of delivery, but it's important to utilize someone's preferred communication style to have effective conflict resolution.

As far as communication with a Two, because it's very important for them to feel heard and be able to express themselves, creating a safe space for them to voice their opinions can go a long way. That can mean reminding them you like them for who they are and actively listening when they release some of their emotional pressure.

Overall, be gentle with the Two and affirm you are seeking resolution together. After all, for them acceptance is on the line, so it's a big deal if they feel like that is being threatened. Be sure to end the conversation on a positive note and make sure they are given the opportunity to fully express how they feel.

An example of a healthy confrontation they will be more receptive to may go like this:

Hey, I really appreciated your help with _____. It showed that you are a team player, and you did a great job. Can we talk more about ___? I'd like to share my thoughts with you so we can understand one another better.

Choosing a Career as a Type Two

When it comes to choosing a vocation for type Two, there are a lot of options! When you consider the core desire for this type, they are usually seeking relationships, affirmation, and being helpful in whichever role they choose.

Enneagram Twos will put their needs on the back burner to support others, so they often excel in an assistant or helper role and can be very fulfilled by this kind of work. This doesn't mean they have to be in an assistant role, though. The combination of their warm personality, desire to help, and ability to connect with people is something that is very valuable and needed in every work environment. Think of writers, activists, social workers, teachers, healthcare workers—all of these are great ideas for fields of work that fit into the core desire of a Two. A counselor is also a great option, but it's important for a Two to have healthy boundaries or they will get lost in the emotions of their clients and "bring their work home" emotionally.

As far as options a Two may not enjoy as much, something that requires a certain amount of confrontation comes to mind, such as a lawyer or a disciplinarian at a school.

Another thing to think about is the work environment. If it's a place of coldness and individualism, they may not thrive. Because of that, modeling and acting may be tough careers for a Two to enjoy. They could be talented in these areas, but they might feel discouraged by the lack of warmth and encouragement in these competitive fields.

Regardless of the actual role, if a Two feels like they are able to make a difference and allow people to feel supported and seen, they will thrive!

Type Twos and Faith

When it comes to faith, type Twos can find it challenging to truly trust that they are not only wanted by God, but actively pursued by him. While they search for that feeling in earthly relationships, it's something that's impossible to find and fulfill outside of the Father.

It's difficult for a Two to rest in their faith because they can't do anything to earn God's love. While flattery and favors win humans over, that doesn't work with God. He loves us just because we are his, which can feel confusing or hard to grasp as a Two. They think, "How can someone want me if I haven't done anything for them?" The truth is, Jesus died for us because of how much he wants and loves us, so let that sink in if you're struggling to really believe it. Imagine your name in Jesus's mind as he made the ultimate sacrifice. We are all forgiven because of the greatest act of love in history.

How can you start to believe you are wanted and loved? Spend time in your own style of prayer as you communicate with God. Maybe it's a journaling kind of prayer, a prayer walk, a prayer drive, or a musical prayer. Find what it looks like in your life, and then stick to that practice so you can regularly hear from the Lord and remember his love for you.

Type Twos in Love

Twos are warm and affectionate, which makes for a comforting relationship. They're usually positive and hopeful as a result, which can be refreshing in moments of hardship or struggle. They are a strong support system for their partner, letting them express how they feel and creating a safe space for their vulnerability. Twos also forgive easily and move on quickly after an argument to restore harmony.

Twos are typically fun and passionate, but they can get lost in their partner's emotions if they aren't careful. They will almost always think of the other person's needs before their own, which is great . . . until they expect the same in return and don't always get it right away.

They often believe the other person can read their mind. This can lead to frustration and unspoken expectations that should be addressed. When the Two can give love freely without expectation, it's the best kind of love!

If you are a Two in a relationship, pay attention to your tendency to get overinvolved with your partner's life, absorbing their interests as if they were your own. It's great to have shared interests, but don't forget to focus on your own hobbies as well.

If you are in a relationship with a Two, let them know how much you appreciate their effort and help in the relationship. Help them define their own needs and boundaries so they are able to stay healthy and fulfilled. Twos are highly empathetic and care about your feelings, so be open and honest with them about your needs and try to be understanding of their perspective as well.

Type Twos with Family and Friends

In the last chapter, we talked about how our family members or those closest to us often see a side of us that no one else does. We named this the shadow side. It's when we let our guard down and feel the most secure. This security can bring out character-istics we didn't even know we had, or we maybe didn't want to admit.

For an Enneagram Two, their shadow side may exhibit the unhealthy traits of a type Four, which can be temperamental, moody, and focused on themselves. They may blow things out of proportion and make false assumptions based on people's actions, which can lead to an argument.

When they're in this space, they are open in sharing what they need, which is good, but they tend to do it in a more demanding way because they've been suppressing their needs for so long. For those closest to a Two, instead of feeling pushed away by the Two's attitude, encourage them to communicate feelings and sources of frustration so you'll both be able to mend and move on.

If you have someone in your life who is a Two, here is how you can love and support them well:

1. Know their love language. As a type that pays attention to other people's love languages and tries to cater to them, it's very impactful if theirs is seen and understood.
2. Tell them how much you appreciate their help and every-thing they do for you. They find a lot of their value in how they serve and love others, so let them know you see it. Practically, this could look like picking up or sending their favorite coffee order on their birthday or before a big test. Not only telling them but showing them you remem-bered and are thinking about them will make them feel very loved!
3. Ask them to hang out when it works for their schedule and do something that doesn't require their help. They might offer to drive or something, but providing a space

for them to truly be a participant instead of servant is refreshing for them.

4. If they offer to help you with something, let them. Whether it's homework, practicing for a game or recital, whatever it is, let them help if they offer. Then, refer to point number two.

5. If they say no to something you've asked them to do, applaud them for it! It sounds odd, but it probably took a lot for them to muster up the courage to say that, so showing them that it's okay to have a boundary will be extremely helpful for them.

Advice for Your Type

I'm a Two, and recently I had an unexpected change of plans and realized I wasn't going to make my coffee date with a friend. I was explaining the situation to another friend when she said, "Well, let me help! I'll do what you needed to do, and you can go to coffee, easy as that!"

I honestly froze. As a type Two, I'm the helper, not the one who is helped, right?

I took this opportunity to challenge myself. Instead of insisting I do it myself so I wouldn't inconvenience her, I said, "Okay, thank you so much!" It may sound simple, but it was a big deal to me that I let anyone help me do anything. If you are a type Two, next time someone asks if they can help you, let them. Instead of feeling guilty or seeing yourself as a burden, remember they're probably offering to help you because they know you would do the same for them.

A Letter to an Enneagram Two

Dear Two,

I see you hiding your needs, not sharing what's on your heart so you don't burden others. I hear your silence when someone asks how you're doing. I know you feel like you can't say no when a favor is asked, but my friend, you can.

You can protect your time, heart, and resources. You don't have to put out your flame so someone else's burns. I know, easier said than done, but you can be loved regardless. You are worthy of love just because you exist. You can ask for help, Helper. You can be the recipient instead of the giver and accept help without feeling guilty or worrying about reciprocating. You can create and maintain boundaries. Yes, you can.

You are loved for who you are, not just what you do. Remember this, dear Two.

Are you a type Two? Before we move on to the next type, there's one thing I want you to know. You are wanted and loved by God. Jesus died for YOU and loves YOU unconditionally. Remember to draw closer to him when you're feeling depleted. Walk in confidence, dear Two, knowing you are wanted and loved just as you are.

Have you learned something new in this chapter? In the lines below, write down what you don't want to forget about this type and answer the following reflection questions:

In what ways do you embody type Two? Are your habits more of a healthy Two or an unhealthy Two?

_____

_____

In what ways do you differ from type Two?

_____

_____

Do you know anyone who seems to fit type Two? How might you encourage them toward healthy Two habits?

_____

_____

What's something you can take from this chapter and apply to your life?

_____

_____

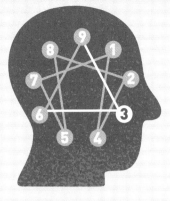

CHAPTER 3

Type Three:
THE HEROIC LEADER

You Might Be a Three If . . .

1. You're naturally a great leader.
2. You don't have time to name emotions because there are more important things to get done.
3. You're competitive to a fault.
4. You're a "chameleon" and can naturally mirror the personality of the person in front of you.
5. You're a master at multitasking.
6. Any failure, even a small one, haunts you.
7. You have a gift of persuasion and could sell wood to a forest.
8. You pay attention to how people respond to you in conversation.
9. You love setting goals and checking off your to-do list.
10. You don't mind shortcuts if it gets something done more efficiently.

Examples of an Enneagram Three

Justin set his alarm for five a.m. to start his triathlon training. He'd planned out the weeks carefully so his workouts would have him in perfect shape for the big event. He had a goal in mind, which was to beat his previous triathlon time, and started his exercises.

With each day, he felt more and more confident. Until, that is, a neighbor on his dorm floor mentioned signing up for the same event. They talked about their training, and Justin realized his neighbor's timing was better in every event. They were faster and seemed more prepared than he was. And it was their *sixth* triathlon. It was only Justin's second!

Suddenly, his confidence started shrinking and self-doubt crept in. The next morning, Justin trained harder than he ever had. He exhausted himself, pushing himself to the limit. He crushed some times he hadn't planned to beat until much closer to race day.

Accomplishment dripped off him like water from the pool, but when his energy was zapped the next day, he grew frustrated and confused. Why couldn't he perform as well as he did the day before? Where would that put him on his training schedule?

He finally realized that getting swept up in competition with someone else was hurting him rather than helping him. Thankfully, by the day of the race, he decided that beating his previous time was enough to be proud of and stopped comparing his journey to his neighbor's.

Kennedy is junior class president and cheerleading captain. She's also on the yearbook committee and has a five-year plan ready for after she graduates. If she's not working on her tumbling passes, she's studying or networking to prepare for college applications, which are right around the corner.

After a day of midterms, a student council meeting, and cheer practice, she plopped onto the couch and put on her favorite show. But instead of relaxing, she started running through a mental list of more things she had to do: "I need to finish the superlatives page for the yearbook, do my homework, clean my room, firm up weekend plans with Kara, and revise my application essay."

Never mind she was exhausted after her busy day; the need to be productive was still tugging at her, so much so that she completely tuned out the show she was watching.

What Makes Up a Type Three?

The Enneagram Three is known as the Achiever or the Performer. They are charming, ambitious, personable, and energetic. They are highly driven to achieve their goals, and in doing so impress those around them. This Enneagram type is often referred to as a chameleon because they can adjust their personality based on the person they're talking to, often mirroring that person's personality. Someone may tell a Three, "I love chatting with you. You just have a great personality!" and the Three may think, "Thanks, it's yours," because of the way they are able to read and respond to the person.

Enneagram Threes typically carry themselves with confidence and self-assurance and are seen as driven and successful, making them a role model for others. But deep down, Threes can be overly concerned with their image and their need to convince others they are doing well, leading them to project the appearance they have everything figured out. Inside, they also often wonder, "Who am I, really?" because of how frequently they "perform" for others. This can then lead them to have difficulty relaxing and being their true selves. Another struggle they may endure is trying to compartmentalize their emotions so they don't have to feel them. They try to "logic" their way out of what they are feeling as an act of self-preservation and safety from whatever they feel is a threat. The problem is, this just buries the emotion, and it ends up popping up at another time, which can catch them off guard.

It's important for Threes to strike a balance between their desire for success and the need to be true to themselves. One thing to note when it comes to Threes is that while a non-Three may hear the word *success* and think it only has to do with grades or getting into their dream school, to the Three it really is whatever the definition of success is to them. So it may not be specific to work or academic achievements, but also how they are doing in sports, relationships, etc.

Their **core fear** is failing or being worthless. They fear being exposed for not being as valuable as they want to be, and this can cause them to put on an act or hide who they truly are from those around them. They often find "micro victories" throughout the day to prove to themselves (and those around them) they are not a failure. When they are hanging out with friends, colleagues, or classmates, they often try to prove their worth to others by adding something to a discussion topic, making sure those people feel that they are a valuable member of the group.

The Enneagram Three's **wounding childhood message** is "You should be who others want you to be instead of who you truly are" or "You're loved because of your performance." Whether indirectly or directly, they were made to believe that they were only worthy of love if they excel in every area of life, which created a drive for success because they feared they wouldn't be loved for who they really are. So when a Three inevitably meets failure in life, they are filled with shame and believe they aren't as lovable. You may see them work harder and give themselves less grace the next time they try the task. It's important to remind Threes they are loved for who they are, not what they can achieve.

Their **core desire** is to feel valuable or worthy. The tricky thing with Threes is that they desire to be truly successful and achieve personal and professional goals, but as long as they *appear* to be successful, it's usually enough to satisfy them. Though they will always fear being found out if it's not authentic success.

They deeply desire to be loved for the person behind the performance, but this may feel impossible if they don't know who they actually are, leading to a spiral of self-doubt and losing themselves in their own facade. That's why Threes need to be careful they're not deceiving themselves into believing the false image they portray to those around them. One great thing Threes can do for themselves is discovering their identity outside of what they accomplish.

The Different Levels of a Type Three

The **healthy Three** is able to accept themselves for who they are rather than what they can achieve. They are able to take off the mask that made them what they thought they needed to be so they can show up as their authentic selves. Because of their natural leadership abilities, this sets an example for those around them to do the same.

Knowing who they are in Christ gives them permission to effectively self-improve and face emotions they may have previously compartmentalized. Rest becomes possible, and the crippling need to perform is silenced.

So if you think you could be a Three, how can you work toward becoming the healthiest version of yourself?

1. Instead of bragging about successes or achievements, be honest about some of the challenges you've had to overcome and how they've made you feel. People are not only drawn to authenticity, they also like a story of triumph, so don't hesitate to share all aspects of your journey. You'll find that your leadership skills sharpen and relationships deepen when you allow yourself to be vulnerable.

2. Take time to rest in a way that truly refuels you. Reading a book, taking a nap, spending the day at the beach, or having a great meal with friends is a good way to actually rest. School, work, goals, whatever it is—it can wait. If you have trouble coming up with ideas on how to rest, do more of what you loved as a child. Were you intrigued by nature? Did you love painting or skateboarding? Staying connected with what you loved then can keep you grounded now.

3. Find time each day to check on someone you love. This will get you out of your own head and into the lives of others. Another way to get out of your own head is to volunteer for a cause you enjoy. Pick something you're passionate about, then find an organization you can work with to make a difference.

4. Pay attention to your coping patterns and feelings when you're in a painful situation. Are you compartmentalizing at all? Find a counselor or therapist to guide you through processing tough things so you can authentically cope with them.

5. When you get too caught up in other people's opinions, practice one of Brené Brown's exercises. On a sticky note, write down the names of five people you love and trust completely, and keep it somewhere you'll see it frequently. Those are the people who get to speak into your life, and it's their feedback you take to heart, no one else's. So if a stranger on the internet posts something mean about you, you won't be as shaken by it, because it isn't from someone on your sticky note. The same is true for when someone praises you. Don't let your ego get swooped up in the praises of anyone not on that sticky note. Make sure those people you list can be real with you and already love you for who you are.

The **average Three** is driven by achieving their goals because, in their mind, their self-worth depends on it. They are naturally good at leadership things like encouraging and coaching others, but the pressure to be in charge and on top of everything can be crippling when they feel like a fraud themselves. While they are efficient, their emotions can be detached, and they may portray a false image of themselves. As a result, they lose themselves to the person they think they're expected or desired to be, while simultaneously desiring to be their true self. They're likely to compare themselves to others, which causes them to outwardly inflate their successes and move farther away from authenticity.

The **unhealthy Three** fears exposure and failure, which feels humiliating to them. They will avoid this at all costs, doing whatever it takes to appear successful to those around them they want to impress, whether the accomplishments are true or not. They become jealous of others, which leads them to be opportunistic and exploitative, sabotaging people who threaten their idea of success. In addition, they can become obsessive and, in extreme cases, narcissistic.

When under stress, Threes show the unhealthy attributes of a type Nine in how they behave and how they feel. This causes them to "numb out" and hide all their emotions and feelings as if they stuck them in a drawer. They may become passive-aggressive or apathetic toward a person or situation. The once-social Three wants to be alone and isolate themselves, typically in a blanket burrito (possibly one that actually looks like a tortilla) while they do something like watch TV. If they aren't in a blanket burrito, they may be found running around, trying to look busy so people don't think they are slacking. The drive and desire they once had to achieve has dimmed and their sense of self is lost.

When in a season of growth, they show the healthy attributes of a type Six in how they behave and how they feel. They become an incredible team player who isn't only focused on their own success but also the success of others around them. The need for competition subsides, and they truly want to do what's best for everyone because they're finally able to think of others and consider how to serve them well, instead of focusing on their own needs and desires. They are able to be more vulnerable and admit they aren't perfect, and that two is better than one. A Three asking for help is a sure sign of health! Finally, they can rest in knowing they are loved just because they are, not because of what they can accomplish. What a sigh of relief!

The **wings** for the Enneagram Three are type Two and Four—the Helper and the Unique Creative. (Recall that wings are the types on either side of your main type, and they add a little flavor to your personality!) The Three with a wing Two is a naturally confident person who attracts people to them with their charm and flattery. They are usually great leaders because they are success oriented but also very relational, so people are drawn to them like magnets! They find efficient solutions to problems and have an admirable dedication to achieving whatever goal is set before them, whether personal or professional. They desire to be liked by all and may manipulate a person or a situation to get there if needed. Another thing they have to watch out for is being overly competitive or possessive and letting that consume them.

The Three with a wing Four is more focused on authenticity and self-awareness. It's a struggle for them, though, because the Three wants to be whatever image is needed in the moment, and the Four wing wants an authentic approach, so it can feel like an internal tug of war on their identity. In their work, they're usually more creative and focused on professional development, and desire affirmation in that space. Always striving for improvement, they may be buried in books or things that inspire them. When faced with difficulty, they're more likely to doubt their abilities and take loss harder than a Three with a wing Two.

Getting Along with a Type Three

We have another case of conflict avoidance in a type Three, although you may not always guess it! The reason type Threes typically mirror the personality of the person they are speaking to is because they want to be accepted and desire a friendly environment (though maybe with a dash of competition on most days).

As a result, using the compliment sandwich we talked about with type Twos is helpful when looking for **conflict resolution**. However, Threes can usually handle more direct feedback, so maybe one compliment with the feedback will suffice. They aren't afraid of encountering a challenge while working on something, but they are concerned with the relationship and their image, so they want to make sure those are not at stake during the process.

Be clear about what you're communicating and use a kind tone, keeping it focused and efficient. Threes value efficiency and want to get to the solution quickly, so come ready to resolve! And as we discussed earlier, they can easily compartmentalize their emotions, so if it's a conversation that may be emotional, make sure they know you expect to hear about how they are feeling so they can think about it as you talk together. Threes may struggle with active listening as well, which is why I'd recommend an environment with few distractions. Don't disturb them while they are focused on a task, and try to find a private setting so they won't be looking around, wondering what people will be thinking.

An example of a healthy confrontation that they will be more receptive to may go like this:

Hey, great job with ____ You get things done so efficiently, and I appreciate that. Can we talk about ____? I'd like to share my thoughts with you so we can problem-solve together and find a route where we all win.

Choosing a Career as a Type Three

The career choice options for an Enneagram Three are truly endless. Because they have an innate desire to achieve, as long as the position has opportunity for advancement and a path to climb the ladder, a Three will probably excel. This results-driven type will thrive in a career where they can be a positive asset to a team and receive some type of recognition, whether it be a raise or title advancement. Honestly, even an email recognizing their hard work goes a long way with an Enneagram Three in the workplace or classroom.

Their efficient and ambitious nature could incline them to seek a career in business, finance, motivational speaking, athletics, entertainment, sales, or anything with a focus on leadership. A competitive environment doesn't bother them, and it could actually work to fuel their efforts. Maintaining a healthy work-life balance is challenging for Threes, so making sure they will be able to take time for themselves is something they need to keep in mind when thinking through a potential role.

As far as some jobs that aren't best suited for Threes, I would say a ghostwriter, audio technician, or computer programmer— roles that are usually behind the scenes and don't offer as much instant gratification. But truthfully, as long as a Three has the opportunity for advancement, they can find motivation in that workplace as well.

Type Threes and Faith

As a Three develops their faith, they may get caught up in the appearance of being put together and perfect. This blinds them from seeing the reality of God's kindness and acceptance for who they truly are. When they find their worth in the Lord instead of in the world, they're able to find a love for their true selves they never knew existed and an assurance that freedom from feeling less-than can be found in the Lord, who is dependable and there for them no matter what. Their striving to succeed in the world can cease when God is the focus, because only he provides the ultimate satisfaction of self-love and acceptance.

The faster a Three learns self-acceptance and understands why God made them the way he did, the faster they'll be able to anchor their confidence in that reality instead of other people's opinions. If you're a Three, ask God how he would describe you. I guarantee they are words of affirmation, love, and beauty that you will be able to walk in moving forward. This reminds me of the story in John 4, when Jesus meets a Samaritan woman at the well, explaining to her he can give her Living Water that will satisfy all of her needs so she will never be thirsty again. When a type Three applies the lesson in this story to their own life, they're able to show up to their faith and other areas of life as their imperfect selves, open to receiving what the Lord has for them, no matter what it looks like.

Type Threes in Love

A type Three values their relationships and wants to meet the expectations of their partner. They're not always the most outwardly emotional, but they do feel deeply whether or not they can express it well. They truly strive to have a happy, fulfilling relationship and be the best version of themselves. They're usually very charming and are searching for someone who brings them a level of comfort by accepting them for who they are. They care about how their partner sees them and want to have a fun relationship where they share a common interest or two.

The inability to express their real emotions can be challenging, but the more self-aware a Three is, the less they will have this issue. When healthy, the Three is open to conversation, willing to adapt for the health of the relationship, and sincerely caring. When they are less healthy, they may go out of their way to seek attention or be glued to their phone for social media validation.

If you are a Three in a relationship, pay attention to your

tendency to hide the real version of yourself in order to impress your partner. If you desire authentic love for the person you truly are, then it's up to you to show up in that way. The less you sing your own praises to your date, the less you will have to wonder if they like you or just the things you listed.

Also, if you are a Three who isn't as comfortable with emotions, and your partner brings up something that is making them feel sad or frustrated, ask them first if they want you to just listen or if they're looking for you to help find a solution. It can be easy to skip over the emotion of it all, but that may be what they need support with the most.

If you are in a relationship with a Three, be intentional about pointing out things you see and love in them that have nothing to do with what they have accomplished. It's great to be supportive and congratulatory when they do something impressive, but make sure to highlight the things you love about their character as well. Be understanding of their need to present a polished image to the world, but also encourage them to be authentic and genuine by creating a safe space for them to talk about their feelings or thoughts. I'm married to a Three, and while I'm so proud of him for things he accomplishes at work or around the house, I'm more thankful and charmed by his heart for his family and the thoughtful things he does to stay connected to his friends. I try to remind him of that often instead of only focusing on what he does.

Type Threes with Family and Friends

Our closest friends and family know us, the real us. An Enneagram Three might find that intimidating and comforting all at once. Because not only do they know who we present ourselves to be, they know our shadow side, which comes out around those we feel most secure with.

So what does a type Three's shadow side look like? They're likely to express their frustrations and unlock some emotions they may have been compartmentalizing. Typically, an Enneagram Three doesn't present much negativity, but when their shadow side comes out, they may complain more or demonstrate a more negative outlook on life. Being aware of this is incredibly helpful for a Three so they can work on healing and moving toward health.

If you have someone in your life who is a Three, here is how you can love and support them well:

1. Tell them you are proud of them. They are probably hoping you are seeing their hard work and achievements, so let them know you do.
2. Dream with them and help brainstorm action steps for those dreams to become a reality. This could look like creating a vision board together!
3. Remind them you love them for who they are, not just what they accomplish. If they feel like they are failing in an area or have failed, show up for them with extra support so they know they are loved regardless of performance. If they're burned out but still refusing to relax, like Kennedy's example at the beginning of the chapter, ask to do something low-key with them so they can take a breath and slow down. A steady friend who sees them for who they are is like gold.
4. Create an intentional day of rest together. Whether it's going to the beach, on a hike, or to a movie, help them leave the striving behind and chill.

5. Don't interrupt while they are working on something or when they are busy, but remember to ask how that task went or how it's going when they are done for the day. They value efficiency, which is why they don't want to be interrupted, but they do want to invite you into their work or project, so talking to them about it is a bonding opportunity.

Advice for Your Type

One thing an Enneagram Three can struggle with is constantly feeling like they need to be striving toward their goals, or that everything they do has to be productive in some way. I want to challenge you, type Three, to set aside at least one day each month (ideally one day each week, but baby steps) to do nothing.

Yep, I mean nothing. Don't do anything productive. Use this day to reset and rest. This is so contradictory to your habits, but you will be amazed at the clarity it'll bring. Not only will it give you a much-needed break, you'll see that people who love you will still love you even when you're not doing something amazing.

I recently challenged my Enneagram Three husband to do this, and he said it was way harder than he thought it would be. Just sitting on the couch and watching TV seems easy, but he was soon itching to go on a run or check off something on his list. But at the end of that day of rest, he felt relaxed and reset.

A Letter to an Enneagram Three

Dear Three,

So you've crossed the finish line; now what? Isn't that the scary part? The "Now what?" Now, rest. Rest to renew your soul, and remember productivity doesn't earn love. You are loved and worthy just because you exist. Yes, just for being you. I know your trophy case's shelves are starting to shake with the weight, but I promise, even if it was empty or you never earned another award, you'd still be valued the same.

I see you turning into the person others want you to be, but your beauty is uniquely yours. You're more than the person you're presenting for approval. Listen, don't look to the left or the right. Look in the mirror and love who you see. You are an inspiring role model, and we are thankful for your example and encouragement to be the best we can be. Now, dear Three, rest.

Are you a type Three? Before we move on to the next type, there's one thing I want you to know. Your accomplishments will not earn your way to heaven; that will only happen through Christ. Allow that weight to be lifted as you learn you are so valued and loved that Jesus died for you, and allow yourself to rest your identity in him as his child. Walk in confidence, dear Three, that you are more than enough, just as you are.

Have you learned something new in this chapter? In the lines below, write down what you don't want to forget about this type and answer the following reflection questions:

In what ways do you embody type Three? Are your habits more of a healthy Three or an unhealthy Three?

_____

_____

In what ways do you differ from type Three?

_____

_____

Do you know anyone who seems to fit type Three? How might you encourage them toward healthy Three habits?

_____

_____

What's something you can take from this chapter and apply to your life?

_____

_____

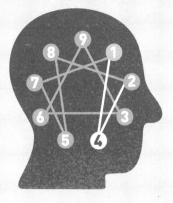

CHAPTER 4

Type Four:
THE UNIQUE CREATIVE

You Might Be a Four If . . .

1. You are generally self-aware and understand your feelings well.
2. Some people say your feelings are too much or too intense.
3. Sometimes you fall off the map for a few days and go silent.
4. You often feel misunderstood.
5. You hate small talk and want to go deep in conversation, even if it's with someone you just met.
6. If something is "what everyone is doing" or trendy, you want no part of it. Being unique is very important to you.
7. You don't avoid sad or melancholy emotions.
8. You are creatively gifted.
9. You can over-romanticize situations or relationships.
10. If someone tells you what to do, you probably want to do the opposite.

Examples of an Enneagram Four

Jake booked a trip to Italy to celebrate graduating from college, and he couldn't have been more excited. He counted down the days, imagined all of the scenery and beauty he would soon experience, and made sure his wardrobe was set so he didn't look too "touristy."

He planned boat excursions, pasta tastings, a tour of the Colosseum, and so much more. But the actual trip didn't live up to the one in his mind. His luggage was lost, excursions got cancelled due to weather, and he almost missed his connecting flight to Lake Como. The disappointment was so overwhelming that he spent an entire day sulking in his villa overlooking the Amalfi Coast. The teal ocean shimmered in the sunlight, but he couldn't appreciate it. Blinded by sadness, his afternoon espresso was flavorless, and all he could do was dream about the flawless trip with no hang-ups or hiccups that he wasn't getting. Instead of savoring the amazing views or delicious coffee, he let his disappointment consume him and it put a damper on his entire vacation.

Gennean hosted a Friendsgiving that was absolutely Instagramworthy. Her curated holiday playlist pulsed through the speakers, and the lights were at the perfect level to welcome comfortable conversation. The table was set, and the handmade centerpiece pulled everything together perfectly. She even included some thought-provoking conversation starters at each place setting. There was only one problem: everyone knew Josh and Katie were in a fight, but they were pretending like everything was okay, faking pleasantries and avoiding the palpable tension in the room.

As the mood became heavier than a weighted blanket, Gennean grew frustrated at watching the performance they were putting on. "If they would just talk it out and resolve things, we could actually get to a good conversation instead of silently walking on eggshells with surface-level topics," she thought to herself. She realized she had to get her thoughts on paper, so she excused herself from the table and made a quick journal in the notes app on her phone.

She felt better after it was all typed out and was able to go back to the dinner and stay present, understanding it was their business to sort out. She started reading some of the conversation starters, and the answers allowed everyone to loosen up, feel present, and have a great time. She even noticed Josh's and Katie's answers to some of the questions started mending their feud right there, even if they didn't come out and say it. The comforting environment she created helped bridge a communication gap, achieving the authentic connection she wanted for herself and everyone else.

What Makes Up a Type Four?

Type Fours are known as the Individualist, the Romantic, or the Creative. They're super interesting people because each person strives for a unique identity, creating their own brand of "them." Usually this type can be harder to identify than others because they don't want to be like anyone else, so one Four can have different preferences or "vibes" than another Four. Male Fours can be even more challenging to identify because they generally want to live in their emotions, but society tells them to do the opposite—so I always commend a male Four when they do lean into the authentic emotions they experience.

Overall, a Four is usually the person who appreciates the aesthetic or vibe of a room or person. Type Fours are deep feelers and can't stand small talk, so don't be surprised if you get a deep question thrown at you within the first five minutes of meeting them. The faster you become vulnerable with them, the more connected they feel. They value authenticity and creativity, which makes them fascinating people in general. Your Enneagram Four friend is likely shopping at thrift stores, finding the craziest piece of jewelry, and pulling off a style you wouldn't dare attempt.

They do, however, struggle with always feeling like something is inherently wrong with them, creating insecurity and anxiety within. They can be emotionally demanding, self-absorbed, and dramatic. They may think the world revolves around them, which can cause a strain on their relationships. I have a friend who is a Four and almost always expects our friend group to do what she wants when she wants to do it, and she gets offended if we don't bend to her preferences. That is an example of an unhealthy Four, which we will learn more about soon.

Their **core fear** is that they have no identity or significance in the world, eventually leaving this planet with their name forgotten and having made no change to society. That of course isn't true, because they impact the people around them in a beautiful way, but it certainly is a fear of theirs. To combat this fear, they work hard in setting themselves apart, focusing on creative self-expression.

There is also a fear in them of being inauthentic, because they are always searching for their true identity. A Four has idealized a person or identity they dream of becoming and constantly compare themselves to that. When they fail to become that "dream person," they begin to question who they really are and what is wrong with them that is keeping them from becoming that person.

The little Four's **wounding childhood message** is "You are simultaneously too much and not enough" or "You will be forgotten if you aren't unique." As children, they likely didn't see similarities to their character and behaviors in their parents or caregivers. This caused them to feel like something was inherently wrong with them, and the feeling of loneliness drove their emotions. They wondered if other people could see all their flaws, and if they also felt like the Four didn't belong.

Their **core desire** is to have an identity and be known for something. They long to find themselves and find self-expression. I mentioned before that they are searching for the ideal self. Because of this search and the disconnection it puts between who they are and who they want to be, they feel like they aren't really their true self. This creates a desire in them to find their authentic self as a unique, creative, special person, and for other people to love them for being that person.

I recently heard an old interview that Dolly Parton did with Barbara Walters. While I personally think Dolly may be a Two, she did say something that sounds so much like a Four that I'm on the fence. When Barbara asked, "Do you ever feel like people make fun of you?" Dolly replied, "Oh, I know they make fun of me, but the joke isn't on me, it's on the public. I know what I'm doing, and I can change it at any time."

I love this because it shows that she's confident in herself and that she's consciously creating a unique identity for herself, which she's done successfully throughout her career. While I haven't personally spoken to Dolly about this, it seems to me she has not only made her music her art but her identity as well. I wonder if this is her searching for her authentic self, or if she has already found and achieved her idealized self. Okay, maybe she could be a Four after all!

The Different Levels of a Type Four

The **healthy Four** is grounded in their emotions and able to reflect on who they are and who they want to be in a productive, positive way. They're reflective, compassionate, creative, and intuitive to the needs of those around them. Emotionally honest, they can begin to see beauty in every situation and circumstance, potentially turning it into art so others can grasp the idea as well. Able to let go of envy, they stop comparing themselves to others and understand God did not make a mistake when creating them. They give the gift of vulnerability to those who need it, modeling the healthiest way to process emotions.

If you think you may be a Four, a few ways to become your healthiest self are:

1. Put yourself in places of joy and positivity, whether that means creatively expressing yourself, getting out in nature, or doing something that will bring out the best in you. You deserve a high level of self-confidence!

2. Get out and try something new instead of waiting for inspiration to strike you. The search for identity is usually aided by doing something creative, so you can not only discover if you're gifted in that area or not, you can find out more about who you really are when you discover what you like and dislike in the world. Do you come to life when organizing your day or connecting with a friend at a coffee shop? Pay attention to those gifts and operate in them. Authenticity isn't felt unless it's lived.

3. Avoid procrastinating until you are "feeling it." Self-discipline is your friend. Make a schedule for yourself and try to stick to it. Whether it's creating working hours for yourself and following them or getting enough rest

or exercise, keeping to a routine can actually shape your freedom and make room for a fullness you never knew before.

4. Try to anchor yourself in what is actually happening instead of the ideas and fantasies in your mind that focus on what you wish life was like. Avoid fictional conversations, arguments, or scenarios that may be over-romanticized. Stay grounded. One way to stay grounded is to spend a few minutes with your bare feet in the grass each day (there's some science to this—look it up if you're curious!).

5. Chat with a counselor or therapist about facts versus feelings and how you can work on leaning more on facts than how you are feeling in a moment or situation. You are stronger than you give yourself credit for!

The **average Four** can become overwhelmed and all-encompassed by their fantasies and ideas, which they eventually believe to be reality. The disconnection to the real world causes them to believe they are inherently different and can live differently than everyone else. "I'm the exception to the rule" could be their catchphrase. They have a deep awareness of emotions, and sometimes it causes them to internalize so much that they take things personally even when they shouldn't. This causes them to become moody, self-absorbed, and dramatic. Often, they then isolate in order to process everything going on inside.

The **unhealthy Four** alienates others and isolates themselves to keep people from thinking they have failed to become the person they want to be. They seethe with envy that others seem to know who they are, and their loneliness tells them that no one will understand them. Once they're in this emotional place, one small thing going wrong can feel extremely big and debilitating to them. When this happens, they shut the world out and don't accept help from anyone. The negative emotions turn from frustration to shame to depression to absolute torture. They could be paralyzed and unable to be productive and sulk in the darkness they feel surrounds them.

When under stress, the Four shows unhealthy attributes of a type Two in how they behave and how they feel. They may become clingy to attempt to manipulate people into loving them. They can be possessive and crave constant attention from the person they are seeking love or validation from. This could be dangerous, as it can breed a codependent relationship and provide a false sense of true love. In extreme cases, Fours in stress can feel entitled and try to force those around them into doing what they want them to do, whatever that may be.

When in a season of growth, the Four shows healthy attributes of a type One in how they behave and how they feel. They are able to keep a routine and see things from a more objective point of view. Not only that, but their productivity skyrockets, and they're able to finish what they need to get done instead of thinking about something they'd rather be doing. They know ways to ground themselves and stay in the present, letting fact lead instead of emotion. Their search for the ideal self is not as urgent because they finally become patient and loving toward the person they see in the mirror.

This process is pretty challenging for a Four, but it can bring great relief once they master it. It's important for the Four to remember how inconsistent feelings can be, so acting on them can be a slippery slope. I have a few Four friends who feel like they aren't as efficient with their work when they aren't feeling it, or like they can't be productive unless they are "in the zone." When a Four is in growth, they are able to get through what they need to get done efficiently, regardless of whether or not they're feeling it, because they can grasp the discipline the task requires.

The **wings** for this type are Three and Five—the Heroic Leader and the Deep Thinker. As we've covered in earlier chapters, wings are the types on either side of your main type and they add a little flavor to your personality! A Four with a wing Three is generally more interpersonal and goal-oriented. Likely more extroverted as well, they are great with people and have an upbeat disposition. They may be more driven by emotion than a Four with a wing Five, and they sometimes feel like their emotions are all over the place. The struggle of this type/wing combination is that they are at odds with each other, just like the Three with a wing Four. The Four in them desires authenticity, but the Three wing seeks approval from others and validation in their accomplishments.

The Four with a wing Five is more withdrawn and mysterious. You may wonder what is going on in their heads or where they disappeared to. They can leave a party without saying goodbye or even stop communicating for a few months even when everything is fine between you. Their isolation is a battery recharge so they can protect their emotions and show up as their most unique self. They typically aren't as image-focused as a Four with a wing Three, so they aren't super concerned with what people think of them or how they show up. Their cerebral nature mixed with the unique vision that comes with being a Four can make for some incredible ideations and creations!

Getting Along with a Four

When it comes to **conflict resolution**, you may have to tread lightly with an Enneagram Four, making sure they know exactly what "size" issue you're dealing with. Many times, a Four can make things into a bigger deal than they may be to the other person, so be clear about where you stand when it comes to the importance of the matter and how it is affecting you. Emotions are a Four's language, so focusing on how certain things make you feel is very helpful for them.

Fours appreciate honesty and authenticity, so don't try to beat around the bush or offer empty compliments to pass the time. During a conversation, make eye contact and give them nods of understanding, and make sure your listening ears are on. Active listening is a big deal, and while this is universally true, it's extra important for Fours because it will feel like an authentic resolution effort, making it extremely effective in helping resolve matters.

Allow them to feel heard, and if they are making a bigger deal out of something than you think it should be, don't shame them or make them feel ridiculous for it. Hold space for their emotions about the situation. If there is one thing you should never say during a heated discussion with a Four, it is, "Ugh, you're just so sensitive." This feels like a knife to the heart and will just escalate things further. Instead, create an open discussion and welcome their emotions.

An example of a healthy confrontation with a Four may go like this:

"Hey, I really appreciate when you did ____ and showed me a new way of doing things. You have a unique perspective, and I appreciate that. Can we talk more about ____? I'd like to hear how you feel about it and find a creative solution together."

Choosing a Career as a Type Four

A few gifts that an Enneagram Four brings to any work environment are depth, creativity, and inspiration. When I think of a type

Four, I think of cool murals on the sides of buildings or the person that does the Anthropologie window installations, because that is some creative stuff! Of course, they aren't *only* creative. They're really motivated by freedom of expression in a role and are usually open to new ideas or abstract ways of doing things.

Vision is very important to them, which makes jobs in industries like fashion, art, design, or entertainment particularly interesting to them. A Five wing may even enjoy politics or business! While this type of job may sound extroverted for a Four with a wing Five, it can be attractive to them because of the freedom of expression and the ability to make a difference in the world, creating a unique identity for themselves. I have a Four friend who works as a travel planner and blogger, which is fun because not only does she use her creative energy to build experiences for other people, she gets to go out and live her amazing trips too!

The roles I wouldn't necessarily suggest for a type Four are ones like an accountant, lab technician, or executive assistant. The lack of innovation and creativity wouldn't be motivational for them in the workplace. Overall, if an Enneagram Four has work that inspires them and allows them to put their own personal touch on it, they will thrive.

Type Fours and Faith

It's important for Fours to recognize who they are trying to define themselves as. Are they following the world and their own idea of the ideal person, or are they able to rest in who God created them to be? Are they placing their identity in their creativity or in God's creation? Searching for oneself without being rooted in the peace of God's love can put you on an emotional roller coaster.

The thing that can bring healing and hope to a Four is remembering God doesn't make mistakes, so they are not a mistake. Their unique gifts, talents, and perspectives were designed intentionally and beautifully.

Consider the words *son* or *daughter* and how impactful those words really are. Children are treasured by their families, and God treasures his children a million times more than anyone could ever comprehend. The gravity of God sending his Son to die for us can ground a Four's faith and allow them to walk in freedom.

When a type Four meditates on the magnitude of God's love, they're able to believe their unique, authentic self is whole and perfect, just as it is, without conditions. God wants you to know you are seen and treasured for all that you are.

Type Fours in Love

The Enneagram Four is full of passion and romance, producing over-the-top ways to celebrate their partner and make them feel loved. They feel deeply, and sometimes can lose themselves in the ideal fantasy of what they want the relationship to be like versus what it actually is. They seek safety in expressing their emotions and want to provide that safe space for others as well. Since small talk is miserable to them and deep conversations make them come alive, asking thought-provoking questions and getting to know them beyond the surface is incredibly valuable.

A friend of mine heard a song that deeply resonated with him, and he asked his girlfriend if she would just sit and listen to it with him. It helped him feel seen and loved that she took the time to appreciate something that moved him. If you feel like you can't match a Four's emotion or intensity, just let them know you aren't able to at the moment, but will try to meet them where they are every now and then.

Sometimes Fours can overly idealize the relationship and end up in their own imagination, ignoring their partner completely. False narratives dance in their minds, and this can start to morph their reality. The Four's passion can bubble over into an explosive reaction to something that may seem small or ridiculous, which can lead to an argument. It's important for Fours (and their partners) to stay grounded in the present.

If you are a Four in a relationship, pay attention to the present moment with your person and the beauty you see right in front of you. Do not succumb to the fear they will abandon or leave you, causing you to put up your guard and start pushing them away when nothing is actually going wrong. They are likely loving you in the best way they know how, even if it looks different than the way you love them. When thinking of ways to spend time together, make sure you take interest in what they would like to do. I know some things people enjoy are boring to you, but it's important to value what is meaningful to them and give them a chance to share it—just like you'd want them to do with you. You might even discover something in the process that inspires both of you!

Similarly, if you are in a relationship with a type Four, support their form of self-expression or art by engaging in the things they enjoy. If your Four is interested in art, visit a gallery together or create your own photoshoot. Learning more about what they're interested in will help them feel seen, and you'll get to have an adventure too! Also empathize with their feelings, even the sad ones, so they feel understood and supported, much like my friend did in the example above.

Type Fours with Family and Friends

A type Four may be more critical or judgmental toward those closest to them when they are comfortable and let their shadow side show. Not only those closest to them, but themselves too. They seem to show unhealthy traits of a type One by becoming more controlling and impatient with any flaws they notice. They can't hide it if they feel displeased with something or someone, which can lead to high tension and a lot of frustration from both parties. They may become more demanding and vocal about their disappointments. Fours, pay attention to the critical thoughts that arise and try to refocus them on the positive aspects of those you love.

If you have someone in your life who is a Four, here is how you can love and support them well:

1. Tell them how much you appreciate their unique perspective and view on things. They want to stand out from the crowd, so highlight when they do!
2. They don't always need cheering up. Fours aren't afraid of feelings, so if they're in their feelings, let them be and offer to sit with them through it all, appreciating their bravery when it comes to facing emotions.
3. Give them a sentimental gift—write letters, record a video, make a playlist—something thoughtful that the Four can keep forever and look back on. This will mean a lot to them and make them feel known.
4. Plan a unique activity that may include a creative element! You could try going to a thrift shop and find each other outfits for the day or do a scavenger hunt with a group of friends.
5. If you find they are falling into a critical or judgmental tone, redirect the conversation by asking what they are working

on that they love right now or ask what has inspired them lately. This will help turn the conversation to something that gives them positive feelings and sparks some joy.

Advice for Your Type

Fours, in order to love yourself and those around you better, do a "self-scan" every day. What do you need to do to take care of your mental health and emotions? What can you do to set "future you" up for success? Maybe it's setting out your clothes for the next day so you don't stress getting ready, or putting down a book that is causing you to get swept up in a fantasy that leads to disappointment when your real life doesn't measure up.

Pay attention to where your actions are leading your emotions. Are you doing something that creates peace in your life, or are you getting caught up in comparing yourself to others? Are you carving out time for a creative outlet, or are you consumed with what you "should" be doing? Whenever possible, choose to engage with things that will foster healthier emotions.

A Letter to an Enneagram Four

Dear Four,

I see what you've made around you. The beauty in a world that's completely yours—unique and complete. When people see your gifts, they are in awe; they treasure the deep conversations and the safe way you hold their emotions. Four, you are golden. You are entirely your own, as set apart as a fingerprint, as twinkling as the stars above. You burn with passion and love fiercely, and you are loved just as much in return. You don't have to love only your potential—you're allowed to love yourself as you are. I promise you are incredible just as you are. Please don't shut the world out when you feel down. There are hands reaching to help you up, to lift your chin, to be the safe place you are to others. Dear Four, release the past and move into the present.

Are you a type Four? Before we move on to the next type, there's one thing I want you to know. When the Lord sees you, he truly sees you. He created you on purpose, for a purpose, and knows exactly who you are. He loves you so much. Walk in confidence, dear Four, that you are seen and understood just as you are.

Have you learned something new in this chapter? In the lines below, write down what you don't want to forget about this type and answer the following reflection questions:

In what ways do you embody type Four? Are your habits more of a healthy Four or an unhealthy Four?

_____

_____

In what ways do you differ from type Four?

_____

_____

Do you know anyone who seems to fit type Four? How might you encourage them toward healthy Four habits?

_____

_____

What's something you can take from this chapter and apply to your life?

_____

_____

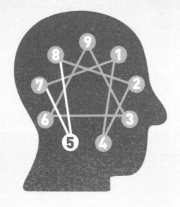

CHAPTER 5

Type Five:
THE DEEP THINKER

You Might Be a Five If . . .

1. You often feel awkward when you're in a group of people.
2. You are a fact-over-feeling kind of person.
3. You would rather observe than participate.
4. You are naturally independent and can take care of yourself. You often wish other people were more like that as well.
5. Because you are a private person, you don't like when people ask too many questions about your personal life.
6. You may need a couple of days to process a situation.
7. New information is exciting, and you love to keep your mind busy.
8. You're not focused on material possessions. You have fewer possessions than most people.
9. You often feel like you need to protect your time and energy.
10. You are a great listener and a "vault" for what people tell you.

Examples of an Enneagram Five

Jaymi's friend Byron invited her to a party. She initially said no, but he challenged her to get out of her comfort zone and finally convinced her to join him. When they arrived at the party, Jaymi's defenses shot up. She started analyzing everything and sorting through her mind's file cabinet of facts when any conversation began. She felt like that was the only way she could prove she belonged in the group.

After about an hour, she was exhausted. She requested they leave and explained to Byron how tired she was. He asked if she wanted to do something else, but what she really needed was time alone reading her favorite novel. He dropped her off at home, and she spent the rest of the evening doing just that.

She felt bad for asking him to leave, but she appreciated he was willing to do so. Knowing that Byron was a plant guy, she went out and got a small cactus for him. She left it on his doorstep with a note that said, *Thank you for getting me out of my comfort zone and bringing me back to it when I needed to recharge my battery. I appreciate you "sticking" with me!*

Taylor and Megan became fast friends during sorority recruitment. They bonded as they went through the process, even though they had different interests—Megan was a communications major and Taylor was pre-med. Taylor had just gotten back from a medical mission trip before the semester started, which fascinated Megan. Anytime they talked, Taylor seemed to know a little bit about everything—she was full of facts about the most obscure topics. Megan always sat on the edge of her seat when talking to Taylor because she knew she was about to learn something cool.

One day, she asked Taylor to hang out, but Taylor said, "I

can't—my twin is coming to town, so I'm going to have lunch with her."

"I'm sorry, *what?*" Megan exclaimed. "We have known each other for three months now. How did I not know you were a *twin*?!"

Suddenly, Megan realized she didn't know anything about Taylor's personal life. She knew Taylor was smart and full of facts, but not where was she from or what her middle name was. Withholding personal information was something Taylor did often, and Megan hadn't even realized her friend was doing it.

What Makes Up a Type Five?

Type Fives are known as the Investigator, the Observer, and the Thinker. They are incredibly cerebral and have an insatiable thirst for knowledge. They love to learn something new and are unafraid to make decisions, since they're usually based in logic or fact.

Because they feel like they have to protect their limited resources and energy, they are typically more introverted and prefer to be alone rather than at a party or in a large crowd. They have amazing attention to detail, which allows them to solve problems easily and work efficiently. They're great at figuring things out, because if you ask a Five a question and they don't know the answer, they're quick to find it! At their best, they are truly pioneers of innovation and unique ideas.

The struggle of being a type Five is the isolation they often resort to as a means of protecting their energy. During this alone time, they are likely studying up on something or creating ideas and opinions—and if they're not careful, that can give them a superiority complex. They can cling to this sense of being smarter than others and become stubborn if they don't keep their mind open to other's ideas or opinions. This can put a strain on their relationships, because those around them feel pushed away and ignored. A Five needs to know they can share their burdens with others and that the sum of their worth isn't in the knowledge they hold. They are loved for who they are, and their needs can be shared without fear of abandonment.

The Five's **core fear** is being useless or helpless. They use knowledge as a defense mechanism, hiding behind facts to protect their vulnerability. This applies to both emotional and physical vulnerability. On the physical side, they feel like if they know everything about their environment, they will be protected from any threats that may come up. And emotionally, many times they don't feel comfortable or welcome in the world around them, so knowing everything they can about a topic helps them feel like they belong.

The Five's **wounding childhood message** is "You're a square peg in a round hole everywhere you go." They have often felt rejected by their peers and even their parents, so they are usually observers who spend a lot of time processing before they build up confidence to express themselves. The message they've internalized is, "The more you know, the higher your value," so learning everything they can about something allows them to feel a sense of self-worth and achievement.

Their **core desire** is to be competent and capable. They pride themselves on their independence and not needing much from anyone. This comes out in their hyperefficient problem-solving, but it can also make it difficult for an Enneagram Five to ask for help or admit when they don't know something. This can leave them struggling without anyone knowing what they're going through and feeling trapped in their own mind. Vulnerability is a challenge, but if a Five trusts you and believes you are a safe person for them, they are able to let their guard down a bit and express their need for help. It's very important for them to not feel like their privacy is being invaded, so be sure not to pressure them for answers if they aren't ready to talk about what might be going on.

The Different Levels of a Type Five

A **healthy Five** is someone who is engaged in life, rather than isolated. They're aware of their emotions and able to express them with their inner circle. They are able to experience life in a deeper way and appreciate the full picture of it instead of limiting themselves to their knowledge and comfort zones. They contribute to the world with incredible new insights, inventions, and innovations that can change the course of history. Sounds lofty, but it's true! Their thirst for knowledge and gift for observation allows them to see things others miss, and therefore create things no one else would dream of. At their healthiest, they can embrace emotions, ideas, and spontaneity, and they come alive as if painted with vibrant color.

If you think you are a Five, try the below steps to become the healthiest version of yourself:

1. Make sure you have a physical outlet to relieve stress and tension. Exercises such as yoga or jogging can be great ways for you to get out of your head and get your physical body moving, so let loose and give your mind a break.
2. Don't just observe your life—live it! Using your thoughts, knowledge, and ideas to disconnect from the present is an escape tactic that isn't always beneficial. Instead, work on being present where you are. One way to do this is to schedule something fun where it's easy to stay grounded in the moment, like a trivia night with friends where you can all share your knowledge and just have fun.
3. The next time you feel stressed or overwhelmed, don't

disappear to be alone. Instead, take that opportunity to let someone you trust know how you're feeling and connect with them. Allow them to be a safe space so you're able to stay engaged with the world around you. Isolation is not the healthiest thing, and it's important not to avoid relationships and emotional attachment.

4. Work on not letting the need for knowledge drive your self-esteem. You are worthy just because you exist, and your needs are not a problem.

5. Talk to a counselor or therapist about various situations and relationships that you feel could benefit from an outside perspective. Sometimes your attachment to information and ideas can cause you to cement your decision, unwilling to hear someone out. Allow a professional to offer a few different perspectives that give you a more well-rounded view of something.

The **average Five** is easily overwhelmed by social settings and tends to live life on the outskirts. They bloom among the wallflowers, and it takes a lot for them to trust anyone. I wouldn't recommend throwing them a surprise party, as they usually hate surprises or being caught off guard in general. They tend to need a lot of privacy and have a social battery that drains very quickly. This is to protect their inner resources, as they live so much in their head.

They lean heavily on facts and tend to ignore or push aside their feelings. The reason they try to ignore feelings is because they fear getting rejected or overwhelming someone if they share their needs with them. This is a big hurdle for them to overcome. One of my Five friends always leads with, "Are you able to help me carry something today?" before she asks for any help, because she doesn't want to be overwhelming. My answer is always yes.

The **unhealthy Five** tends to have thoughts they cannot control, which prevents them from accessing their emotions. Highly fact-driven, they second-guess if they have enough resources (emotional bandwidth, social battery, etc.) and isolate in order to protect themselves at all costs. This causes them to become hostile if someone invades or interrupts their time alone. They may become perfectionistic or critical of themselves. Usually, in this space, their mind theorizes and haunts them, distorting reality. Their life becomes a secret to those around them, even their inner circle.

When under stress, a Five shows the unhealthy attributes of a Seven in how they behave and how they feel. They begin to feel scattered and restless, filling their time with random things instead of productive and focused tasks. They may begin to grow impatient with people and add too many things to their plates all at once. They end up giving themselves so much to juggle that responsibilities start to fall between their fingertips. Usually, when overwhelmed or stressed, a Five will start talking faster and include details unrelated to the conversation.

When in a season of growth, a Five shows the healthy attributes of an Eight in how they behave and how they feel. They exude confidence and tend to be more physically active, going on walks or to the gym. Growth allows them to spend less time in their head and more time actually doing the things that have been processing up there for a while. Courage allows them to be more social and feel like the best version of themselves. You will see them truly engaged in the world around them and excelling in every area of their lives.

The **wings** they have are type Four and type Six—the Unique Creative and the Loyalist. As a reminder, wings are the types on either side of your main type and they add a little flavor to your personality! A Five with a Four wing is typically more emotional and creative, able to feel emotions deeply and channel them into something concrete. A friend of mine is a Five with a wing Four, and she's an incredible songwriter with a lot of depth and detail in each of her songs. She often writes alone, which is a common behavior of this combination. They may detach from others because they're more sensitive than many people realize. Whether it's writing a screenplay or breaking new ground in their area of expertise, they are highly creative and intelligent. This wing type is often mistyped as a Four, but paying attention to the core motivator is the key to differentiating the two.

A Five with a Six wing is usually more cerebral than emotional, struggling with deep interpersonal connection yet still desiring it. The Five part of them wants to stay emotionless, while the Six part of them wants to create a network of safe relationships. Both parts of them desire to master something and understand it clearly, so they're better at solving problems and analyzing data.

Both wings have an incredible ability to look at things with new perspectives, and if I had to guess, I'd say that many murder mystery writers are a Five with balanced wings. Can someone call Rian Johnson and confirm?

Getting Along with a Type Five

While a Five can keep to themselves a lot, they really are amazing people to have in your corner. One way to instantly connect with a Five is to take an interest in the area they have become an expert in. I enjoy learning about things people love and why they love them, so even if it's not something I'm naturally drawn to, I'm usually fascinated by the obscure facts Fives are easily able to recall. Fives are great at igniting others' curiosity by bringing something unique to the table, which can set you up to discover even more information.

As far as **conflict resolution** goes, I highly recommend not bringing up a hard conversation out of nowhere. Give the Five a heads-up that you'd like to talk and then come to them with clarity and rationalization.

If you remember the compliment sandwich from chapter 2, you can go ahead and throw that sandwich out of the window here because Fives don't need it. Since Fives are knowledge-based, they need logical facts and practical solutions to resolve a situation or conflict.

Focus less on the emotion of it and more on the cause and effect of the matter. While it's helpful for a Five to feel some emotions and empathize with the person bringing something to their attention, it'll likely take a minute before that process happens, so I'd recommend not bringing emotions into the conversation until the facts are presented.

As their social or conversational battery may die quickly, be efficient with explaining how this issue affects you and what you need from them; they will file it inside their mental filing cabinet in the drawer that has your name on it.

An example of a healthy confrontation that a Five will be more receptive to may go like this:

Hey, if now's a good time, I'm hoping we can talk more about ____. I'd like to learn more about your thought process and strategies and share my thoughts with you so we can problem-solve together.

Choosing a Career as a Type Five

If you have a project that you want completed efficiently, creatively, and quickly, call an Enneagram Five. They thrive on lo-fi music and productivity, and their curious nature mixed with their gifts of problem-solving and innovation empowers them to find unique solutions to any problem. Specifically with a Five who has a wing Six, I tend to think of someone at NASA. Their observations help them work efficiently and with incredible attention to detail, and they're also great in a team brainstorming environment.

I personally work with an Enneagram Five, and the way she thinks of things that never cross my mind and tends to details I totally would've missed is truly amazing. Like most Fives, she often doubts herself and her abilities, only to blow my mind with what she can create and how innovative she is. Fives can habitually sell themselves short, but they bring so many gifts to any path they choose.

Fives start to feel less motivated when they feel misunderstood, ignored, or underutilized. They hate being seen as if they don't have much to bring to the table. They thrive when working alone and may be interested in the career fields of philosophy, physics, engineering, business, or computer programming. Overall, if an Enneagram Five's work allows them to solve problems, they will succeed.

I mentioned earlier that I think many murder mystery writers could be Fives, and I want to reiterate that because when you consider a Five, you may not think about that kind of creativity, but that is something they can thrive in. While it takes a bit more tapping into, it's cool to see what they come up with.

That said, there are some careers that an Enneagram Five may not love. I wouldn't necessarily suggest jobs in retail, wedding planning, or public relations, as these are typically very social jobs that may drain the Five's battery quickly.

Regardless of what career path they choose, if they're able to use their thorough and critical thinking, Fives will thrive.

Type Fives and Faith

As far as a Five's relationship with faith goes, it can be challenging for them to trust that they don't have to be self-sufficient and can lean on the people around them for strength. Not only is their community there to support them, but the God of the universe is too!

While there are plenty of scientific and historic facts about Jesus' life, miracles, and Christianity, the nuance aspects of faith that are rooted more in feeling than observable fact (like the Holy Spirit and God's guidance in our lives) are often a struggle for Fives. But when they grasp the whole picture of how the two sides work together to support the reality and love of God, they're able to walk in the freedom that an intimate relationship with God brings. They can lower their defenses and allow the satisfaction of life with the Father to wash over them.

In their faith journey, Fives might be especially interested in reading resources that contain facts and historical accounts that help ground deeper elements of faith, such as works by Lee Strobel or C. S. Lewis. When I think about Fives and faith, I'm reminded of Christ being called the "Good Shepherd" and how closely a shepherd watches over his flock, tending to them and providing for their needs. Psalm 95 talks about us being his sheep, which means God is tending to us, providing for our needs so we have all of the resources we need to thrive. God wants the Enneagram Five to know they are loved and provided for in every way through him.

Type Fives in Love

Fives in a romantic relationship might surprise you, because despite being more logical than emotional, they are very attentive to their partner and will be able to be very present when they are together. Not only that, but the attention to detail they have when it comes to gift-giving often allows their partner to really feel seen and understood. They're great at observing their partner's preferences and will give a gift that shows this!

As a cerebral type, Fives want someone they can have intelligent conversations with who also respects their need for privacy and alone time when they need to recharge. The struggle they may run into is in expressing their emotions. Because of their logical mind, the emotional side of a relationship can be harder to access and explore for them.

If you are a Five in a relationship, try to think through how the other person may be feeling or receiving information. What emotions are rising up in them? What emotions are rising up in you? Do not suppress them or try and think through them; just feel them. As independent as you are, know that it's okay if you let your guard down a bit and allow someone in, sharing how a situation makes you feel instead of just what you are analyzing about it.

If you are in a relationship with a type Five, give them the space they need to rest and process (which can be often!). This can even look like being in the same space but not interacting. Fives value the kind of relationship where they can coexist and still maintain some independence. That doesn't mean they want to sit in silence all of the time, of course, but it's nice every now and then.

Adjusting to change and being in social settings for too long can be overwhelming for Fives, so be mindful of these things as they come up. Last but not least, be sure to engage in thought-provoking conversations with them. What is something you're learning about right now that you could learn together? They will love exploring something new with you!

Type Fives with Family and Friends

When it comes to people we feel most loved by and safe with, we tend to exhibit some different behaviors than normal. When Fives are in this position, they can start to exhibit some traits of an unhealthy Eight as part of their shadow side. Typically, a more isolated Five will suddenly be more aggressive and interject their "expertise" into conversations. They'll feel compelled to debate any facts they feel you have incorrect, creating tension from their argumentative reaction.

Fives, pay attention when you start to feel the desire to provoke someone, so you can take time for yourself to return to a neutral position.

If you have someone in your life who is a Five, here is how you can love and support them well:

1. Take an interest in whatever they are focused on learning about at the moment. Ask them questions about it and what they learned.
2. Hang out at a museum together or spend an afternoon at their favorite bookstore.
3. Be okay with silence during your time together. As long as you are being real with them, it doesn't matter if you aren't having a deep conversation. In addition to this, pay attention to when they feel like their social battery is running out. Give them the space they need to recharge.
4. Don't pressure them to talk about their feelings. Respect their privacy, no matter how close you are. They will talk when they are ready as long as you make sure they know they can trust you.
5. Remind them how valuable they are and how much they bring to the table. They want to feel capable and competent, so be specific with your examples.

Advice for Your Type

Fives, I have one tip that will help you connect with others better in your everyday life. This may make your skin crawl, but it will also expand your comfort zone and help you feel warmth from people everywhere you go.

When you're going somewhere, whether it's class or a restaurant or a store, smile at people you pass or sit close to. I know, I know, you don't necessarily want to engage in conversation, but I think you may be pleasantly surprised by the results of this experiment. It's a good way to move from observing the world around you to actually engaging with it, and you could end up having an interesting conversation!

A Letter to an Enneagram Five

Dear Five,

Come closer, lean in, and don't pull away. I know it's tempting to hide when the walls feel like they're caving in, but trust that people love you and want to help. We're in awe of your ability to pick up anything and learn it at lightning speed, but *that* doesn't make us love you. We love you simply because you exist.

It's okay to love logic, but sometimes love is illogical. Set aside the black and white and let the gray blends happen. Lay your armor down and let us in. Try it, just once.

I see you're a master of many things, and that is incredible, but you're worthy without it all. The most beautiful things in life are to be lived. The most wonderful people are waiting to love you. Come closer, dear Five.

Are you a type Five? Before we move on to the next type, there's one thing I want you to know. You can ask the Lord for what you need. He is listening and waiting for you to draw near to him. He wants to bless you, so open your hands to what he has ready to support your weary heart. Walk in confidence, dear Five, and know that you can rest in him.

Have you learned something new in this chapter? In the lines below, write down what you don't want to forget about this type and answer the following reflection questions:

In what ways do you embody type Five? Are your habits more of a healthy Five or an unhealthy Five?

_____

_____

In what ways do you differ from type Five?

_____

_____

Do you know anyone who seems to fit type Five? How might you encourage them toward healthy Five habits?

_____

_____

What's something you can take from this chapter and apply to your life?

_____

_____

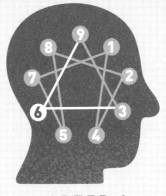

CHAPTER 6

Type Six:
THE LOYALIST

You Might Be a Six If...

1. You are prepared for anything and play out worst-case scenarios in your mind.
2. You are hilarious and witty, but do not crave to be the center of attention.
3. Anxiety is usually a struggle for you, and many people don't understand how intense it is.
4. It's difficult to trust people in authority.
5. You do not like unpredictability, surprises, or a change of plan.
6. Some people think you are pessimistic when you're really just trying to prepare.
7. If something is going too well, you wonder when the other shoe will drop.

8. You don't trust people easily, so you focus on quality in friendships instead of quantity.
9. You're a great friend, cheerleader, and encourager who is likely still friends with people from childhood.
10. You're a great team player and someone who will always pull their weight on a group project or task.

Examples of an Enneagram Six

Jenny, Marissa, and Jess have been friends since middle school. Jenny, an Enneagram Six, is their "glue." She makes sure everyone stays in touch and checks in to see how each person is doing on a regular basis. Jenny has a gift for loving her friends well and making sure they each feel seen and thought of. For birthdays, she gives gifts she knows will make their heart happy, and Marissa and Jess both know they can count on Jenny for absolutely anything.

One time, the three of them got into an argument, and Marissa wasn't sure their friendship would last. While she feared she would lose her two best friends, Jenny stepped in with reassurance she wasn't going anywhere. "One argument won't ruin our friendship if we are sorry and do our best to not let it happen again," she said. They all sighed with relief, apologized, and made plans to go to their favorite frozen yogurt place after class. A few weeks later, their teacher assigned a project about friendship. When asked to describe Jenny, Marissa said, "Loyal and generous," while Jess said, "Steady and hilarious!" It's apparent that these three will be lifelong friends.

Austin City Limits was a week away, and **Daniel** was almost done packing his car for the road trip with Vincent and Tyler. He checked the website again to make sure he knew what to bring. He also researched the best parking and planned out who they would see on what stage and when.

Since Tyler was only packing "vibes" and Vincent always waited until the last minute, Daniel had everything in order for them to have a stress-free, seamless trip to ACL. Taking care of his friends while preparing for any scenario was his specialty.

As they got on the road, they talked about the festival and hyped themselves up for the shows. Suddenly, they heard a loud pop—their tire was flat. Daniel's face turned red as anxiety rose to the surface, thinking about how much time they'd lose, but thankfully he was prepared with a car jack, a spare tire, and a YouTube tutorial.

What Makes Up a Type Six?

Type Sixes are known as the Loyalist, the Skeptic, and the Guardian. They are amazing friends who will stick with you for the long haul, unphased by small arguments or bumps in the road. Sixes are some of the most reliable people you know, as they are committed and have a fierce loyalty to those they love.

They have what sounds like a committee in their minds, offering multiple perspectives, fears, cautions, and foresight, which can create anxiety and cause the Six to be unable to make decisions. They seek safety in relationships and belief systems, yet often have a skeptical relationship with authority figures until trust is earned. Sixes are usually prepared for any outcome due to the "What about this? What about that?" dialogue that goes through their minds.

Many Sixes may read the above thinking their need to feel prepared and question every angle is a negative thing or a problem, especially because the committee in their minds can cause them to worry and feel uneasy, but this trait has positives as well. We really need our Six friends and family members to keep us thinking about what is going on around us and ensuring our safety. Sixes are also able to think quickly and act effectively because they have all the info together and steps planned out. But the challenge for Sixes as they prepare is to trust themselves and the world around them, instead of constantly expecting something to go wrong.

Their **core fear** is being without safety or security, so they seek it out in every area of their lives. This means they crave predictability and plans, which is why they like to have a strategy ready in case something unexpected happens. The fear of feeling fear itself is very real to them, so their overpreparation is an effort to avoid that entirely. The little Six has an intense **wounding childhood message**. They believed from a young age that "It's not okay to feel safe" or "You cannot trust your own judgment." Somewhere along the way, they were led to believe the world is a dangerous place full of uncertain situations and unreliable people. This is what created the "inner committee" I mentioned. If you've ever seen the movie *Inside Out*, the character named Fear can show us a peek into the anxiety Sixes can feel—and let take the controls.

Their **core desire** is to feel safe and secure in every area of life, whether that is in relationships, at work, or in their physical environment. They do this by investing in and fostering relationships that feel safe to them. They essentially build a support system for others so they are able to then lean on that support system.

One other way they feel secure is by finding a strong authority figure to follow. Since they are typically hesitant to trust authority figures, it's rare and extremely comforting to them when they find one. They may also look to external structures and systems—such as a job, a community, or a set of rules—to provide a sense of stability and direction.

There are actually two different types within type Six: phobic and counterphobic. Both of these types share the same core fear and desire, but they differ in how they respond to fear.

When you think of these two types, think of our "fight or flight" instinct. The phobic Six's response to fear is more of a flight instinct, trying to avoid their fear at all costs. The counterphobic Six follows the fight instinct—they see fear and face it head on, trying to quickly overcome it. For this reason, a counterphobic Six can sometimes be mistaken for a type Eight, so it's important to pay attention to the person's core desire and fear to determine their type.

The Different Levels of a Type Six

The **healthy Six** is a champion of those around them, confident in their choices and abilities, resting in the security of their faith. They are loyal and steady, providing the security for themselves they often search for in others. They are less suspicious, allowing them to be more trusting not only of others but of themselves. This shift to a positive mindset brings out self-confidence that people want to follow and brings more inner peace all around.

If this type sounds like you, in order to become the healthiest version of a type Six, check out these steps:

1. Pay attention to your mindset. One thing many of my Six friends struggle with is a scarcity mindset, believing they're at risk of losing something important. "What if it doesn't work out? What if I'm wrong and this isn't what I

think it is?" Work on shifting this mindset one situation at a time. Ask yourself, "What if it *does* work out? What if this *is* what I think it is?" Being intentional about looking on the bright side will allow you a bit more freedom to feel optimism and hope.

2. Do you tend to get on edge when a plan changes or something catches you off guard? Identify the things that cause this reaction and ask why they may be so triggering to you. The edginess can become a spiral of self-doubt and pessimism, which we want to avoid. Once identified, talk through the possibilities with a trusted friend before you get overwhelmed.

3. Talk with a counselor or therapist about the inner committee in your mind that's shouting all of the worst-case scenarios. It is possible to silence them, which will allow you to trust your decision-making and not rely on others for that. The lower you sink into the fearful thoughts, the harder they are to climb out of, so processing with someone who has the tools to aid you will be super helpful!

4. If you're working through fear, know it's okay and you're not alone. Fear in and of itself is not harmful. It gives us warning flags that allow us to take action on a matter and protect ourselves or whatever needs protecting. The problem is when it becomes crippling or debilitating. That's when it needs to be addressed on a different level. Try box breathing (see chapter 1 for what this looks like), counting, or tapping as coping skills you can use as you sort through the fear and how it's making you feel. (And if you're wondering what tapping is, it's when you "tap" points on your body with your fingers while you repeat a positive message, which helps release the stress—research it to learn more!)

5. Choose to believe the best about people, including yourself. Find someone you trust and work on giving them more trust. Then trust someone else, then someone else. Try not to lead with suspicion when it comes to meeting new people. I worked for a church where the lead pastor operated in "high trust, low fear," and that is powerful when it comes to conflict resolution!

The **average Six** tends to be short-tempered as they take on the responsible role of the group, thinking of all of the things that could go wrong or should be avoided. This can lead to some controlling tendencies as they feel like no one else could manage things as well as they can. They navigate a tension between wanting to be able to relax and worrying about all of the things because they believe no one else will.

The **unhealthy Six** is usually very anxious, thinking of worst-case scenarios everywhere they go. They believe they're always in danger or that someone may be out to get them. They begin to lead with suspicion, unsure of whether or not the people around them are actually trustworthy. The fear of being harmed or abandoned gets overwhelming, which makes them push people away and second-guess everyone's motives. Paranoia and defensiveness start to take over, and they entirely lose trust in their own decision-making, trying to figure out what the right move is while feeling like they are alone and scared.

When under stress, the Six shows unhealthy attributes of a type Three in how they behave and how they feel. This detail about Sixes is so interesting to me because I wouldn't assume this would be their reaction to stress, but it is! A stressed Six becomes arrogant and opportunistic because they are worried about what people think about them. As a result, they will become more competitive and try to avoid failure at all costs. Failure is unavoidable, of course, but they can't see that in this state. Unlike the healthy version of themselves, they begin to worry how people may judge them and how they look appearance-wise, so charm becomes a strategy to gain loyalty, just like an unhealthy Three.

When in a season of growth, the Six shows healthy attributes of a type Nine in how they behave and how they feel. The racing thoughts slow down and they can actually relax. When this happens, they're able to be more present and enjoy where they are in real time.

The most amazing thing that happens in growth is that the once codependent Six begins to trust their own judgment and stand on their own two feet, finding security and safety within themselves. Because they stop looking for external guidance and validation, they can move forward in confidence, trusting their own reasoning and thoughts. This allows them to create deeper relationships and offer that same security to those around them. They are finally able to discern when it's time to hold on and when it's time to let go.

The **wings Sixes** have are types Five and Seven—the Deep Thinker and the Adventurer. Remember, wings are on either side of your main type and add a little flavor to your personality!

A Six with a type Five wing is typically more cerebral and introverted. Knowledge is very valuable to them, which allows them to think more objectively than many people. They are often hard-working and more cautious than a Six with a Seven wing. The Five in them has an independent streak, but the Six in them remains loyal to those they love and respect. This makes them amazing for group projects because they are a team player and great at getting their part of the job done. Highly analytical, they value debates and conversations that make them think. They are efficient problem solvers, but they may struggle with isolation when their own problems arise, shutting people out and not communicating well. When that happens, they could be seen as cold or distant.

A Six with a type Seven wing is usually more extroverted and friendly, collecting friends and keeping their relationships tight so they feel safe. They typically are down for an adventure and extremely prepared for anything that could go wrong during said adventure. They're the friend who will join you for a camping trip or music festival and bring all the gear you need to have the most fun experience!

This type combination is surprisingly good at keeping their word or commitment. While the Seven side of them gets hesitant, the Six in them values the relationship so much that they will make it a priority. When struggling, they may be more anxious and reactive, unable to make a quick decision. They can also seek assurance from those around them either through self-deprecating humor or just asking where they stand in your friendship.

Getting Along with a Type Six

As far as **conflict resolution**, an Enneagram Six appreciates a warm, genuine approach. Because this type typically has the worst-case scenario at the top of their mind, if anything is at stake, make sure they know up-front so they are aware of what they are actually dealing with. They also need to feel heard and like they have fully expressed themselves by the end of the conversation.

As a security-seeking type, the more reassurance you can give them throughout the conflict, the better. How can you make them feel safe and positive with the topic at hand? Remember, they have an inner committee firing off a ton of thoughts all at once, so don't rush them to process what they are thinking and feeling. After they process what was communicated, they may want to revisit certain aspects of the conversation, so allow them the time they need to feel confident in moving forward. You will gain their trust by being trustworthy and consistent, so be sure they don't hear about this conflict from anyone else before you bring it to them to resolve. I'd recommend taking a "together" approach when resolving any issue because Sixes are great team players and want what's best for everyone.

An example of a healthy confrontation that a Six will be receptive to may go like this:

Hey, thank you so much for _____ I so appreciate that you are a team player. Can I ask you more about _____? I'd like to hear the options you've thought through and better understand so we can find a solution together.

Choosing a Career as a Type Six

Sixes are great for keeping an organization or business in tip-top shape. Not only do they provide organization and devotion, but because they are phenomenal team players, they'll bring people together and help collaborate on ideas or visions. They have the amazing ability to provide security and stability in their work, and they genuinely want what's best for the team.

They're motivated by helping others, so being able to trust their coworkers is really important to them. They do not appreciate when their feedback is ignored or if the expectations for the projects aren't made clear.

Sixes are great at administrative work and keeping things in order. Other fields that may interest an Enneagram Six are teaching, banking, occupational therapy, or environmental health. An Enneagram Six would also make a great vet if they're an animal lover!

There are some roles I wouldn't recommend for a type Six, though. A freelance position may be tough on them due to the lack of coworkers or a team environment. The same could be said for an accountant or programmer role. Cutthroat careers like sales or recruitment may not be favorable either.

Overall, if you give an Enneagram Six a work environment where they can be a part of a united team, their tasks will be completed with excellence.

Type Sixes and Faith

Faith can be an incredibly comforting and safe place for an Enneagram Six to rest. It gives them an important anchor and a way to hold on to hope in the midst of their worries and concerns. When they are walking in faith, they won't feel the need to predict and prepare for what's next because they have the security of their Creator.

There is always unpredictability in life because we are human and each of us have free will, so it can be hard for Sixes to keep steady when things don't go smoothly and suspicions and doubt flood their minds. But their "what ifs" can be silenced by trusting in God and taking their anxieties to him. When they're able to do this, they are more confident and trusting of their own discernment when it comes to decision-making. True freedom is found in faith. God wants the Enneagram Six to know that they are safe and secure in every way through him.

Type Sixes in Love

When it comes to love, a type Six isn't called the Loyalist for nothing! They're incredibly faithful and devoted to their partner, providing that person with the safety and security they also desire. They're very loving and often trustworthy, bringing comfort to their partner as well.

Because they are typically slow to trust, it's a big deal when you earn the confidence of a type Six. But some serious struggle will occur in the relationship if the Six feels betrayed or their trust is broken. Since it took so much for them to trust in the first place, seeing that trust broken is monumental and could cause them to react by becoming more controlling, affecting the health of the relationship. It can take a long time for their trust to be earned back as they work through suspicion, which can be frustrating to the other person.

They will likely be pretty transparent in the early stages of your relationship because they want to know if they can have confidence in you and if you will be as invested in the relationship as they are. If you aren't, they want to know as soon as possible so they know how high to raise their guard and/or if they even want to keep investing in a dating relationship. If they are in an unhealthy place, they may end up self-sabotaging because they constantly wait for the "other shoe to drop," which can lead to them to constantly ask if everything is okay or if you still love them. This is a search for safety and security, so either reassure them the relationship is solid or be honest with them about its status.

Sixes, make sure you are working on maintaining your self-confidence so these doubts don't take over and turn into anxieties you end up acting on. Don't try to test your partner, pulling them in and then pushing them out to test their loyalty. I know it's easier said than done, but if you do your best to operate from a place of trust, you may find some peace in that place when it comes to relationships.

If you are in a relationship with a type Six, you may be the chief decision-maker and captain reassurer. Be ready to take leadership in those areas so they see you as a safe person they can count on. Your optimism can inspire theirs! They will likely love inside jokes and being goofy together—Sixes often have an awesome sense of humor. You could even make up a game together, inventing your own rules and just enjoying the silliness that ensues. Quality time is valuable to a Six, and that is one fun way to have it!

Another idea is to make a consistent day of the week "your day," where you do something like going to get smoothies together or hanging out at a park with lunch in tow. Spending intentional time with your Six will go a long way in helping them feel secure and loved.

Lastly and probably most importantly, do not dismiss their worries or fears. I don't recommend saying "calm down" or "relax" to anyone when they are bringing a problem to you, but especially not Sixes! Instead, help think through worst-case scenarios with them and come up with solutions to the problem at hand. They are dependable, funny, and caring, and you will see the full extent of that when they feel like they can trust and depend on you.

Type Sixes with Family and Friends

With an Enneagram Six, when they enter their shadow side mode, they may get easily overwhelmed when they're with those they are closest to if they feel like too much is being asked or expected of them. This can cause them to become passive-aggressive and feel like they're being stretched too thin. Because they give so much to their nearest and dearest and are so loyal, it can feel like a lot if they are running on empty and begin to feel taken advantage of.

If they run into any friend or family drama, you may find them shutting down and running away from it to avoid confrontation or any other worst-case scenarios that may be playing in their minds. Sixes, pay attention when you start to feel like you're out of your comfort zone and note how you may be reacting.

If you have someone in your life who is a Six, here is how you can love and support them well:

1. Consistency is extremely valuable to type Sixes. The more consistent you are in your friendship with them, the more loved they will feel. This can look like regular communication and hang outs, or making a point to show up for important dates and events.

2. Initiate a hang out and make the plans so they don't have to. Typically, they are the ones to get everyone together and make everything happen, so take the load off their shoulders and let them relax for a bit.

3. Oftentimes, a type Six is everyone else's biggest cheerleader, so try being a cheerleader for them the next time they need a pep talk. Remind them of a time they were nervous about something and ended up succeeding so they remember that they can trust themselves!

4. Be mindful if they are feeling anxious and ask them how they'd like you to respond. Also, be ready to lighten the mood if they need a little help lifting their spirits! Take them to a fun activity or do something that will facilitate laughter.

5. Offer reassurance often. When a Six asks if you are mad at them or if y'all are okay, don't get frustrated. Instead, offer calm reassurance with a scoop of kindness.

6. Communicate well and show interest in their day, thoughts, plans, and projects. They are typically great communicators who want to include you in their day-to-day lives, so engage with them via text or intentional time at home.

Advice for Your Type

If you're a Six struggling with anxiety, one thing that might be helpful is an exercise called Categories. Did you ever play a game in the swimming pool called the same thing as a kid? It's a similar concept! When you're feeling anxious about something, pick a category (i.e. cars, animals, colors, celebrities, etc.) and list as many things as you can in that category. See how many things you can think of in a few minutes. This technique can help you refocus and ground yourself in the present moment.

A Letter to an Enneagram Six

Dear Six,

"What if this? What if that?" Where would we be without you, dear Six? My question to you is, "What if you trusted yourself, just this time?" What if your worries fell away, your confidence burst forth, and you could rest in the knowledge that you are okay. It is easier said than done, I know, but all you need is within you. Inhale, exhale, and take up your strength to take the next step forward, though it's unknown.

Thank you for keeping us all sane and safe, sweet Six. Thank you for having wide shoulders to carry it all, for showing up every single time we need you. For being the greatest friend a friend could have. For seeing us, for believing us. You can be for yourself who you are for everyone else. Instead of looking for the emergency exit, trust your intuition, dear Six. You are trustworthy to everyone, including yourself.

Are you a type Six? Before we move on to the next type, there's one thing I want you to know. You are safe in the embrace of the Father. Pray Psalm 91 over your life as you seek security. Get to know the voice of God so you can trust what you are hearing from him. Walk in confidence, dear Six, that you are safe in his arms.

Have you learned something new in this chapter? In the lines below, write down what you don't want to forget about this type and answer the following reflection questions:

In what ways do you embody type Six? Are your habits more of a healthy Six or an unhealthy Six?

_____

_____

In what ways do you differ from type Six?

_____

_____

Do you know anyone who seems to fit type Six? How might you encourage them toward healthy Six habits?

_____

_____

What's something you can take from this chapter and apply to your life?

_____

_____

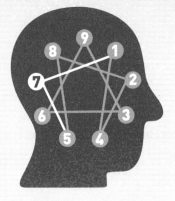

CHAPTER 7

Type Seven:
THE ADVENTURER

You Might Be a Seven If...

1. You are always down for an adventure, even if there is no real plan or itinerary.
2. FOMO (fear of missing out) is a real fear of yours that can lead to overcommitting.
3. Some of your friends and family members may describe you as flaky.
4. If the mood is too heavy, you will tell a joke or do something funny to make people laugh and change the tone.
5. You love variety and try to avoid boredom at all costs.
6. You think people worry more than they should and that everything will be okay.
7. The bright side is the only side!
8. You've picked up a collection of hobbies but have mastered none of them.

9. You struggle with long-term commitment. Whether it's with people or plans, it makes you nervous.
10. You love the idea of the future and all of its endless possibilities.

Examples of an Enneagram Seven

Sarah was scrolling Pinterest one night when she came across a picture of the most beautiful sunrise at the top of a hike. Wanderlust filled her veins and the mountains were calling—she had to go. She booked a flight for the next day. She didn't plan where she would stay and didn't research what she should bring, but she was ready in a moment's notice for an adventure.

The breeze tossed her hair as she made the final few steps to the top, ending up exactly in the spot where the photo had been taken. She'd wanted to catch the sunrise, but her lack of planning caused her to miss the cotton candy sky. The hike had taken a lot longer than she'd expected, and her stomach growled when she reached into her bag and realized she forgot to pack snacks.

I'd love to tell you she still took the time to enjoy the beautiful view, reflecting on the journey behind, the present one, and what was to come, but she had no time for that. She'd made a friend on the flight and was meeting them for lunch. She was already on to the next adventure!

Cole said he wouldn't miss his friend Cade's birthday dinner, but when the night came, he was nowhere to be found. When his friend messaged him the next day asking where he'd been, Cole simply said, "Sorry, bro, I got caught up. Let's celebrate soon!"

Cade texted back right away, pointing out that Cole had bailed the last three times they had plans, and that he'd seen on social media that Cole had gone to a bonfire instead of his birthday dinner. It was true—Cole had lost track of time at the bonfire, and by the time he'd realized his mistake, it was too late to make it to Cade's event.

Cole knew he should apologize, but he didn't want to face the fact Cade was mad at him. Instead, he waited a couple days for Cade to cool down before texting him, "Hey, man, want to hit the gym?"

Cade agreed even though Cole had yet to acknowledge his text. At the gym, Cole acted like nothing happened, but when they grabbed a bite after, he could tell Cade was frustrated. Cole finally explained what had happened and apologized, inviting Cade to hang out later that night. Cade agreed and appreciated the apology.

What Makes Up a Type Seven?

Type Sevens are known as the Enthusiast, the Adventurer, or the Optimist. Think of a human exclamation point. Yep, that's your Seven friend. They are known as the life of the party who always sees the silver lining in every situation. Enthusiasm runs through their veins, and extrovert could be their middle name. They are in awe of the world around them, seeing endless opportunities, which is such a gift to have!

They are often risk-takers who don't feel plans are entirely necessary. "Who needs to plan in advance? Where's the excitement in that?" they may ask. Sometimes I have trouble wrapping my mind around this, but even with all the risks a Seven takes, somehow it usually works out for them. My cousin and two of her friends flew to New York City on a whim one day because she wanted to go to *Saturday Night Live*. They may have had to camp out all night in the rain, enter two different lottery drawings, and take turns getting provisions and taking bathroom breaks, but wouldn't you know it, they got in! Less than twenty-four hours after deciding to go, she and her friends were in the audience for the live show.

Many people wish they were a type Seven, but it's not all sunshine and rainbows, contrary to what they may display. Sevens are so focused on joy and happiness because they have a true fear of missing out and are uncomfortable facing or discussing serious situations or feelings. They often avoid painful feelings by putting them away in a cabinet and focusing on the good, which can cause the situation to get even worse. They can fear commitment, whether it's to a person or to a plan, which can create a shaky trust with those around them or depending on them. There is a constant fear in the back of their mind that something better could come up and they would miss out. The fear of missing out is a real thing for them, so you will rarely find them alone or sedentary.

The Seven's **core fear** is being in pain emotionally or being deprived. The desire to cover up pain by doing fun, distracting things and their fear they'll miss out on something better if they do fully commit to a plan is a tricky tension to navigate, so they may over- or under commit, trying to figure out the most exciting way to spend their time. If they overcommit, they can seem flaky to those involved in the plans they have to bail on, and inadvertently send the message that those people aren't important enough to them. Same for under committing—they can make people feel like they don't value the relationship enough to want to show up, when that isn't the case at all. In the end, the over- and under committing and "adventure distraction" can lead to a further desire to fill an emotional void and avoid boredom.

The Seven's **wounding childhood message** is "Don't pay attention to any negative emotions" or "It's not okay to depend on anyone emotionally." This message was likely directly from a situation where their emotions seemed neglected by someone they trusted, which caused them to neglect their own emotions. As a result, Sevens are always bouncing around from activity to activity, always on the search for the emotional fulfillment that nothing on earth can offer.

For example, a friend of mine was ill in high school and had to be homeschooled for two years while she was in and out of the hospital. Now, as an adult, she fears missing out on anything in life, so she is always doing something exciting, usually with at least one person by her side, making plans for future fun. She wants to avoid the isolated and negative feelings she had so often when we were younger.

Their **core desire** is to be content and satisfied. Being present and grounded really helps fulfill this desire in type Sevens, but it takes practice to recognize the satisfaction it brings. Being where their feet are isn't easy for them, but when they master it, it's incredibly enriching. They crave stimulating experiences, so they don't limit themselves in life. A phrase I think of when I think of the Enneagram Seven is "Everyone, everything, all the time!"

The **healthy Seven** knows the true source of joy and adventure, and searches for it in the Lord instead of in the world. They are in awe of the world around them, seeing beauty in the smallest things and in the hearts of people. They're the kind of people who will gaze into a sunset, noting every color or brushstroke of the Creator.

With their identity firmly planted in God, they can address the hard emotions or dark feelings they've been avoiding. They recognize that pain, sadness, and hardship are normal parts of life that can be processed in a healthy way. While their playfulness never leaves, they are able to be practical and grounded in a new way.

So if this sounds like you, how do you become the healthiest Seven? Try some or all of the ideas in the list below.

1. This may be a hard one, but it'll be very valuable. Learn to live with less external stimulation. I know, I know. Try it, though. Turn off your phone, laptop, and the TV and just sit quietly for a while. Notice how it makes you feel. Are you uncomfortable? Are you antsy? Why do you feel like you always have to have something happening? Learn to listen to your inner dialogue so you can find peace in the silence.

2. If acting out of impulse comes very naturally to you, resist giving in to that urge. For example, if you want to buy something, hold off for a day or two. If you truly can't stop thinking about it, then revisit your decision. As you let the immediate impulses pass, you'll be able to figure out which things are actually worth acting on.

3. Be present where you are. Don't worry about what's next. What is happening now? Enjoy each bite of food on your plate. Pay attention to the nature around you. Listen to the person you're talking to—really, really listen.

4. Talk with a counselor or therapist about the emotions or situations you've been avoiding. They will help you face them in a way that feels doable instead of overwhelming.

5. Commit. Be a person of your word and follow through when you have committed to a friend or loved one. If you have made plans, stick to them. On that note, make the plan. Even if something "better" or "more exciting" comes along, don't let FOMO win.

The **average Seven** is usually trying to create new and exciting experiences to avoid sadness, disappointment, or pain at all costs. They are often constantly searching for the next adventure, and while they can be good at cheering you up, they aren't the friend you go to when you need a shoulder to cry on. They don't always know what to do with serious feelings or what they believe are negative emotions, and living in the present is challenging for them.

Typically, the average Seven has trouble with commitment in relationships or plans in general, and they are the ones who tend to keep plans open just in case something more exciting comes along. The avoidance they cling to doesn't serve them because people start to doubt they'll actually show up emotionally or physically.

The **unhealthy Seven** cannot handle any type of boredom or painful conversation. They usually brush serious things off and dismiss them as unimportant or not worth their energy. This is because the Seven gets freaked out by the heaviness or seriousness of the issue at hand and looks for a way to distract themselves or forget about the situation altogether.

They are extreme risk-takers, sometimes being reckless and throwing all caution to the wind. They believe nothing can go wrong, so they abandon discernment and may end up in a dangerous situation. They're always seeking fun and pleasure, yet they never feel satisfied due to an insatiable need to find something better. They also may struggle with having a short attention span, unable to stay focused on a conversation or sit still very long. This can be frustrating for the person they are with, which will cause the Seven to avoid the negative emotions, starting a cycle of escalating tension.

When under stress, the seven Shows unhealthy attributes of a type One in how they behave and how they feel. They may become perfectionistic and unforgiving of their own and other's mistakes. Their usual carefree nature turns sharply critical and perfectionistic. With nerves suddenly all over the place, their previously open mind turns narrow and closed. Black-and-white thinking clouds their judgment and pessimism creeps in. You may not even recognize them as the same person when they're in a moment or season of stress because the behaviors are so contradictory to who they usually are.

When in a season of growth, the Seven shows the healthy attributes of a type Five in how they behave and how they feel. I love seeing a once-discombobulated Seven show their growth by becoming more collected and organized—and operating at this level often makes the Seven happier as well. They are able to focus on the task at hand or conversation in front of them, instead of searching the room for something or someone more exciting. They are able to shine in both innovation and execution. This can also be surprising to see! One of my friends is a healthy Seven and has a good balance of work and play, which allows him to move into seasons of growth often. Not only is he a professional wakeboarder, he's also a neurosurgeon. Yep, that was not a typo. He can balance the fun and the demand of that work well, most of the time, because of his level of growth.

The **wings** for this type are Six and Eight—the Loyalist and the Challenger. A Seven with a Six wing is typically outgoing and creative, full of passion and fun! They are more impulsive when it comes to discipline and decision-making. They're definitely the kind of friend to call you out of nowhere with an adventure in mind. Focusing more on relationships than a Seven with an Eight wing, they are a fun friend who keeps those around them laughing. When I think of a Seven with a Six wing, I think of someone I want to go white water rafting with, because they will always be down and won't forget the snacks or a change of clothes.

A Seven with an Eight wing is more disciplined and assertive than the wing Six, and they move toward their goals with determination and tenacity. Their confidence is more apparent, and they inspire those around them as they can dust themselves off from any stumble and continue on. With a combination of strategy, optimism, and persistence, they're inspirational to those around them. They usually have an open mind but are direct when needed. When I think of a Seven with an Eight wing, I think of someone who is a class clown and yet always has straight As. How did they manage to ace the test when they were doodling or on Snapchat during class? I was always jealous of this person in high school.

Getting Along with a Type Seven

Okay, the conflict resolution piece for an Enneagram Seven is a big one to understand and navigate well because they will absolutely try to slide the issue under the rug and do something fun instead. They have an escapist tendency when it comes to hard, serious conversations or emotions, so minimizing distractions in the environment around you is helpful when you're having one of these conversations.

It's important to bring up the topic with no accusations or criticism so both of you have freedom to express yourselves. Instead of the compliment sandwich, Sevens prefer a compliment cupcake, where it's a sweet cake of compliments topped with more sweetness and a great time. Even with this complement concoction, their desire for avoidance can lead to tension in the conversation, so try to keep them focused and centered on the issue at hand. They definitely don't want negativity in the relationship, so there is usually a desire to resolve it. Just make sure you get to the point quickly so a resolution can happen as soon as possible.

So keep it short, minimize distractions, and have something fun to talk about afterward so they don't feel like you are both dwelling on the conflict. And if you need more time to process the issue or what you discussed, let them know, because otherwise they'll leave everything in the past.

An example of a healthy confrontation they will be more receptive to may go like this:

Hey, thanks for ＿＿. Can we quickly talk about ＿＿? Then maybe we can go grab a bite together.

Choosing a Career as a Type Seven

If you're looking for an energetic, future-minded employee, look no further than an Enneagram Seven! (If you're looking for attention to detail, maybe keep looking.) The adventurous nature of a Seven is an incredible gift in the workplace, as they are usually the ones to rally the troops to keep morale high and dream big dreams for the workplace.

You might imagine a Seven would thrive as a white water rafting guide or ski instructor, and you'd be right! But they also may enjoy being an interior designer, publicist, flight attendant, fitness instructor, or entrepreneur. A highly relational Seven is all about creating new opportunities and good vibes. Because of their active imaginations, they are amazing at brainstorming and getting people excited about a variety of new ideas.

They may struggle in a workplace if they feel like they aren't part of a team, if there is a rigid routine, or if they feel restricted in their decision-making. I wouldn't necessarily recommend a type Seven apply for a job as a librarian, administrative assistant, or customer service representative. Overall, if you give an Enneagram Seven something to look forward to either within the goal or at the end of it, it will be met.

Type Sevens and Faith

When it comes to faith for a Seven, they may fall into a pattern of relying on experiences for satisfaction instead of the Lord. That's because their insatiable desire for fun and adventure can lead them to emptiness as they search for the satisfaction only Christ can fulfill. The emotions that are required to face our human nature can also cause an Enneagram Seven to struggle, since they want to avoid addressing heavy feelings. However, when we can face our negative emotions and bring them to the Lord, we can move forward with a peace that only confidence in him can bring. Resting in God's presence brings true contentment and joy, exactly what a Seven is searching for. The sadness and despair Sevens avoid can be easier to navigate when they tap into their faith and trust God to help them work through it. The Lord wants the Enneagram Seven to know that a relationship with him is full of adventure. Next time you take a hike through nature, think of God's work as he created the leaves, the dirt below your feet, and the flowers blooming around you. Listen for him in the bird's song and watch his art in the sunsets. Find him in the adventure so you don't feel like a relationship with him and your wanderlust have to be separate.

Type Sevens in Love

When it comes to love, a type Seven brings fun, passion, and freedom that is refreshing and exciting! They show their partner how to find beauty in the small things and that adventure is always one spontaneous decision away. Sevens are usually fascinated by the person they love, wanting to know all about them on a deep level. They are full of questions on a daily basis, excited about anything new that is happening, and always interested in their partner's day-to-day life.

While I absolutely believe there aren't two specific types that go best together and that it's more a case where two healthy types are the best fit, there is one pairing I often see with Sevens—surprisingly, type Ones. This seems to be a classic case of when opposites attract. The Seven feels grounded with a type One, and a type One feels like they can let loose and have fun with a Seven. Pay attention, though, to your seasons of growth and stress if you find yourself in this kind of relationship, as Ones and Sevens are on the same stress/growth line. When a type One is in growth, they show healthy attributes of a type Seven, but when a type Seven is in stress, they show unhealthy attributes of a type One. So these two types—and any pair who share a stress/growth line—have an interesting dynamic. They see the best and worst of themselves in the other person, which can cause tension if there is a lack of self-awareness.

No matter what type you are, trouble may occur in a relationship if the Seven starts to feel trapped. They like to feel grounded but still want to be free, so independence is important to them. As one of my friends always says, someone being "too available" to other people is a red flag. While some independence in a relationship is a good thing, there are times a Seven's desire for freedom can actually be a sign that they're afraid of commitment, which can be frustrating for their partner.

Sevens, when you're in relationships, be aware of your tendency to ignore details or avoid serious conversations and emotions. Sometimes your partner may be trying to tell you they need to have a real talk and your mind is either preoccupied or trying to avoid the hard moment altogether. Do the work it takes to not only face tough topics but also bring them up yourself and be prepared to address them. As fun as it would be, joy is not the only emotion we experience. Have you ever seen a feelings wheel? If not, google it and see just how vast our emotional range is as humans!

If you are in a relationship with a type Seven, be aware of their need to not feel limited or "tied down." Do what you can to help them feel grounded but not trapped. One thing you can try is finding something you both love to do. Do this together *and* independently so you can talk about your experience with it when you come together. Maybe that is volunteering together, rock climbing, or doing the daily Wordle!

Another tip if you are in a relationship with a Seven is to remain chill when they do share some big or heavy emotions with you. They don't want it to be this big dramatic thing—they'd rather just express it, work through it, and move on. So when this happens, take your cues from them and be present, process, and proceed. Then plan something fun to do together!

One date night idea that would be fun after a serious session is geocaching. It's basically a real-life, crowd-sourced treasure hunt—you can use an app to find where people have hidden a box, take something from it, and leave something else behind! It's something you can do just about anywhere, and it will appeal to a Seven's sense of adventure.

Type Sevens with Family and Friends

Our shadow side is the side of us that comes out around the people we feel most loved or secure with—which can mean some unusual actions or emotions come to light when they see the side we usually keep out of view. A type Seven will eventually get tired of being the optimist when they're around those they feel safe with. Sometimes they will want to be alone, or maybe they'll let down their guard and show you a side of them that might seem pessimistic. They may experience some thoughts that cause dread or sadness, which they don't want to face but are suddenly unavoidable. When a Seven becomes an observer in a room instead of an active participant, laughing and carrying on with everyone else, they may be leaning into their shadow side and need some TLC.

Sevens, pay attention to when you start to feel like you want to hide away from the world, and take some time for self-care when it happens. Reach out to a friend, practice a hobby that helps create a routine instead of a rush, or reflect on previous times when you slowed down enough to enjoy the moment.

If you have someone in your life that is a Seven, here is how you can love and support them well:

1. Tell them what you love about their latest project or hobby. Because Sevens tend to hobby hop, jumping from one idea to the next, they can get discouraged easily. (Hence, the hopping to avoid their emotions.) Encourage their efforts in what they are working on so they feel more equipped to stick with it long-term.

2. In addition to talking to them about their new interest, you could also give them something related to that hobby. If it's painting, for example, buy them some new brushes and offer to work on something together! Bonus points if you surprise them with this gift!

3. Spend intentional, quality time with your Seven. They value one-on-one time that deepens the relationship, even if you aren't having a serious conversation. Give them your undivided attention as you hang.

4. Sevens can often get lost in the ideation and anticipation of the future. Dream with them, but help them keep

their feet planted by savoring the moment and being right where they are.

5. Be a safe place for them to express their emotions when they are ready. Encourage them to do so when the time is right, or they will have trouble later when the negative emotions start to pile up. It's important that they feel secure and free to dig deep, because it's not something that comes naturally to them. And be ready to switch the topic to something light or exciting when they are over it, because when they're done, the shift can be abrupt.

Advice for Your Type

I have a couple of productivity hacks for a type Seven that may seem funny, but they will be helpful tools when you need to really focus on a specific thing you need to get done, whether it's in your future career or homework or chores! The first hack is the "Puppy Hack." Just like you do when training a puppy, give yourself a treat after completing tasks that don't give you immediate joy. Whether that treat is a trip to Starbucks, making plans to hang out with a friend later, or watching an episode of your favorite show, it will give you something to look forward to at the end of every task and help you tap into the motivation needed to get it done! Once you're used to this, try doing two tasks before the treat, then three. Eventually, try to finish all of your less-"exciting" work for the day before you get your treat. Soon, you will notice that procrastination isn't as much of a crutch as it once was.

The second hack is "Body Doubling" when you need to complete a task. I got this trick from Justin Gillespie, who is an LMSW in Michigan. If you need to clean your room, have a friend come over and sit while you clean. He calls this "Body Doubling" and says it works to "enhance executive functioning of tedious and sensory overload tasks such as cleaning or organizing." I personally love having someone over while I clean or organize as it helps distract me from the overwhelm of what lays before me. If I know I get to hang out with my friend, it helps the time pass and is a fun distraction! This is such a helpful hack that I'm suddenly realizing I should tell my sister about it . . .

A Letter to an Enneagram Seven

Dear Seven,

Don't be afraid. No, I don't mean don't be afraid of skydiving into your next adventure or trying a new thing. I mean don't be afraid to be still, look into the eyes of a friend, and bare it all. Find a new adventure in the exploration of your emotions. It may not sound as exciting as the five different ideas you have at this moment, but it's much more rewarding for your heart. I know you're the "life of the party," but I see your heart wanting more. Yes, it'll involve some pain, but pain is an important part of life too. Life's lows help you fully appreciate the highs!

Keep inspiring those around you to do the thing they've been wanting to do. Continue to be the light they need as they wonder if they should book the flight or climb the mountain. That comes naturally to you, and it is so, so beautiful. We need it, and we need you. More than your vibrant laugh, we need *you*. We need your heart. We need you to see the awe and wonder in yourself that you see in others. It's easier to avoid, but, dear Seven, don't be afraid.

Are you a type Seven? Before we move on to the next type, there's one thing I want you to know. The God of the universe has your life in his hands and is taking care of all of your needs. You can rest in his arms for contentment, knowing he is providing for you in the mundane and in the adventure. Walk in confidence, dear Seven, that you can find contentment in the Lord.

Have you learned something new in this chapter? In the lines below, write down what you don't want to forget about this type and answer the following reflection questions.

In what ways do you embody type Seven? Are your habits more of a healthy Seven or an unhealthy Seven?

_____

_____

In what ways do you differ from type Seven?

_____

_____

Do you know anyone who seems to fit type Seven? How might you encourage them toward healthy Seven habits?

_____

_____

What's something you can take from this chapter and apply to your life?

_____

_____

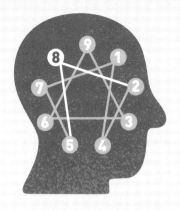

CHAPTER 8

Type Eight:
THE CHALLENGER

You Might Be an Eight If . . .

1. You are quick to defend the vulnerable and believe that justice is worth the fight.
2. Opposition and confrontation do not scare you. In fact, you often welcome it because you think debating is fun!
3. You don't trust people easily.
4. Vulnerability is difficult for you, so you really value the people you can be vulnerable with.
5. You will do anything to protect your loved ones.
6. You've been told you're "too much" or "too aggressive" before.
7. You are skeptical of people you think are too nice.
8. People say they wish they had your confidence.
9. You're not a people-pleaser by nature.
10. You're great in a crisis because you're able to think clearly, stay calm, and consider solutions quickly.

Examples of an Enneagram Eight

Londyn and Celeste were at a store where someone seemed to be following them. As they did their shopping aisle by aisle, in almost every other aisle a guy would pop up out of nowhere, just staring at them. He was wearing sunglasses inside, and when he would pass them, he'd get closer and closer. Londyn was extremely aware of his presence and felt herself going into full protector mode.

As they were checking out, Londyn asked the cashier if there was a person at the store—such as a security guard or a clerk—who could walk them to their car. Celeste was confused and asked, "Why on earth do we need someone to walk us to the car?" In order not to freak Celeste out and have her overreact, Londyn ignored the question and waited for an escort to walk with them through the parking lot. They were making small talk with the security guard as they went to their vehicle.

The man from the store was lurking by their car but snuck away quickly as they approached with the guard. Londyn and the guard noticed he was leaving, and as the guard yelled at him, Londyn turned to Celeste.

"See that guy running?" she asked Celeste. "He was following us while we were in the store."

Londyn turned to the officer, thanked him, and they climbed into the vehicle.

"I'm sorry, *what*?" Celeste exclaimed.

"Stick with me; I've got your back," Londyn said. She turned up the radio and rolled out of the parking lot.

Chris is a tattoo artist who has a dry, sarcastic sense of humor and no room for bull, which he can typically detect from a mile away. It was a normal Tuesday afternoon when Brighton sat in his chair, describing the dainty art she wanted to decorate her forearm. She had a sunny disposition and was as "basic" as basic gets, complete with an iced coffee in hand. Chris rolled his eyes as she described the small size of the tattoo, as if it were a waste of both of their time.

"Tattoos are meant to be seen. Big, with a story," he said.

"It does have a story," said Brighton, "and I just don't want it big. No bigger than a quarter, please."

He scoffed. "Must be an important story if it fits on a quarter, huh?" said with a quirk of his lips. He was not realizing he was slowly but surely pushing her away with his sarcastic humor.

He made one more comment he thought she would laugh at, but when he looked at her, tears were streaming down her face.

"Whoa, whoa, I'm so sorry. I didn't mean to upset you," he said.

"Well, you did," she replied.

His jokes had gone too far and hurt his client. He felt terrible and apologized as best as he could. He ended up not charging her for the work and wrote an apology a few days later, telling her the lessons he had learned.

What Makes Up a Type Eight?

Type Eights are known as the Challenger and the Protector. They are sometimes called "intense" because of their straightforward and honest nature. They are the type with the most energy and a natural self-confidence that is truly inspiring to those around them. Truly, the self-confidence an Eight has is why they are amazing motivational speakers. They will show you that you really can do anything you put your mind to. I always watch in awe as my Eight friends run circles around me when it comes to productivity.

I call Eights jelly beans because despite their tough exterior, they are softies on the inside, especially if you are in their inner circle of people they love and trust. If you've made it to that place with an Enneagram Eight, however, your words and actions can wound them pretty deeply, so pay attention to the weight they give your advice. Many people are easily intimidated by Eights, but when you know they are tender inside, you realize they are easy to love.

They portray a tough exterior for self-preservation because they don't feel like the world is a safe place to be vulnerable and open. The Enneagram Eight is your "tell it like it is" friend, which can be helpful or harmful depending on how they present the information and who they are communicating to. One of the most valuable things I learned about the Eight is that they aren't trying to be hurtful and they don't always know how their tone comes across, so it's important not to take many of the things they say personally. I would even advise you to ask them, "Is that how you feel in general or specifically toward me?" if they say something that seems out of pocket to you.

My favorite thing about Eights is how honest we can be with them. They will be honest in return, and if you're in their inner circle, they will have your back no matter what. Their superpower is being an incredible protector to their friends and family. They're amazing at taking care of those around them in ways that may surprise you. Instead of typical nurturing attributes (like listening, being patient, giving up time), you may find them more physical in their protection. Eights are the ones who will stand up to a bully for you or make sure you don't get overcharged for something. They want you to feel as safe with them as they feel with you.

However, Eights are often called "harsh" and "too much" because of their strong opinions and willingness to speak their mind. This is something that can be true, and it's important to remind your Eight friend that not everyone can handle the intense way they present information. Sometimes unaware in the moment of how they can come across, they might "steam roll" people with their opinions or ideas, which can create tension within the relationship. It's even harder when the Eight is aware of their effect on people and just doesn't care, because in their minds, people should "get over it." It's important for Eights to remember that their words and actions strongly impact those around them, and it's up to them to decide if they want to create peace or harm.

Their **core fear** is losing their power or feeling controlled by their circumstances, environment, or people around them. They are very fearful of being vulnerable because they believe people may take advantage of their vulnerability and use it against them. They cope with this by always needing to be in control. Whether that is being the one who drives places or the person taking the lead in situations and conversations, they will make it known who is in charge. They are more likely to be drawn to people who exude confidence and honesty versus someone who hides their messy feelings or takes a more subtle, manipulative approach. They are the kind of person who is "what you see is what you get," and appreciate that in others as well.

Their **wounding childhood message** is "No one is trust-worthy" or "It's not okay to be vulnerable." Little Eight was forced to be independent far too early. They saw the world as a place to "eat or be eaten," which caused them to rely on survival instincts like a lack of vulnerability or gentleness. The thing is, though, since they are gentle on the inside, the fear of betrayal is hidden deep within them. They have an armor around their hearts to prevent anyone controlling their emotions, but practicing trust can help them find a healthy balance when it comes to allowing vulnerability while keeping boundaries.

On the flip side, their **core desire** is to protect themselves and the ones they love. They defend their nearest and dearest at the drop of a hat, and will be at your side immediately if you need them, ready to defend you in any way you may ask (and even ways you don't). They also protect themselves by seeking independence. This can lead them to reject anything that restricts them, whether it be a person, construct, or idea.

You can often tell by an Eight's leadership if they are in a healthy place or not. The healthier they are, the more encouraging they are. However, the unhealthier they are, the more dictatorial they are toward others. When I was in high school, I had an Eight friend who sat with us every day at lunch. If she had a problem with someone or if she was in an unhealthy place, she would decide someone couldn't sit in our circle. If that sounds like a scene from *Mean Girls*, that's because it sort of was! On days when our friend was healthy and in a good place, though, she was fiercely protective of every single person in that circle. If I knew then what I know now, I think I could've communicated to her well and avoided some serious drama.

The **healthy Eight** is able to let down their guard and allow people past the walls they've built up. They're confident in who they are in Christ and operate in his strength more than their own. Okay, that one can be tough for an Eight, but when they submit to Christ and rely on him, it allows them to be open and compassionate toward others. We love to see a healthy Eight who is able to be more flexible than insistent on their own suggestions and opinions. They become incredible leaders, full of encouragement and inspiring confidence in those they are leading.

If you sense you might be an Eight, here's how you can achieve this confident-yet-soft leadership trait:

1. Recognize you can't do it all on your own. I know it seems like you can because you have energy, drive, and confidence, but who do you turn to when the well runs dry? It's important to have people you trust around you. Find those people and let them support you. It's okay to ask for help.

2. On the topic of letting people support you, know that not everyone is against you. If you do start to believe this, you'll end up isolating yourself and it'll turn into a self-fulfilling prophecy. Welcome in vulnerability to strengthen the relationships in your life.

3. Talk to a counselor or therapist about what to do when people don't "obey" the advice you give them. Focus on the fact you want to lift people up, not just flex your power muscles. You are a great leader when you inspire those around you, not when you try to control them. A counselor can help you reframe your thoughts and find the best way to communicate.

4. Take the idea of power off a pedestal. Power is not what earns respect. Respect earns respect. Consider how you can be more respectful to your loved ones, and you'll see how love grows naturally when you're not trying to force it.

5. Check your ego. Are compliments or critiques going to your head? Don't let the opinions of others shape your self-confidence. Usually, Eights say that they don't care what people think, but I believe this is a self-preservation tool more than the truth. Let both the compliment and critique fall away and leave what the Lord says about who you are.

The **average Eight** is opinionated, even confrontational in their interactions. Impatience can get the best of them as they rush people or processes along, pushing things to the limit. Their frustration can be very apparent, and you'll usually know what's on their mind without asking. Sometimes they start arguments "just because," or in an attempt to gain power or authority over someone or something. This is what makes people intimidated and want to avoid Eights entirely. Overall, the way to describe an average Eight may be "intense, not in a good way."

The **unhealthy Eight** is highly combative and typically dominates their relationships. They become cruel and unable to hold anything back, letting their words cut deep and saying hurtful things to assert their power. They are a "bulldozer," destroying anything in their path. Vulnerability is not an option, and trying to connect with them will feel like trying to connect with a brick wall. In trying to maintain control so that no one can betray them, their controlling demeanor offends those around them, causing them to cut ties or put up a boundary, making the Eight feel betrayed and convinced they were right not to trust people in the first place.

The Different Levels of a Type Eight

When under stress, the Eight shows unhealthy attributes of a type Five in how they behave and how they feel. They will seclude themselves and hide away from everyone. Fearing that their vulnerability is entirely exposed, they will shut everyone out and become fearful. This may result in a cynical view of the world as they detach from their emotions and the people they love. Typically, Eights aren't afraid to take action, but in stress they may feel frozen, with thoughts just running circles in their minds.

When in a season of growth, the Eight shows healthy attributes of a type Two in how they behave and how they feel. They become incredibly empathetic and compassionate, loving those around them with great warmth and gentleness. Showing the softness of the jelly bean, they are honest about their emotions and open up, not feeling so afraid of vulnerability. When they see a need, they meet the need, serving others with their time and attention.

One of my favorite Eights and I were working at a coffee shop when something happened on my website that I didn't know how to fix. They saw the panic wash over me and immediately jumped into action, helping me process what I was feeling and breathe through the worry, and within five minutes they had researched and fixed my issue. The compassion and steadiness they showed me in that moment will stick with me forever.

An Eight's **wings** are type Seven and Nine—the Adventurer and the Gentle Peacemaker—which are on either side of their type and add a little extra to their personalities. The Eight with a type Seven wing has a lot of energy and confidence, allowing them to tackle anything with minimal fear of failure. They are big dreamers and big doers, accomplishing almost everything they put their mind to and inspiring others to do the same. They thrive with the energy of these two types and do things that are both creative and practical.

This type combination may struggle with impatience and become demanding or bossy at times. They may overindulge in an area of life and desire a safe person to keep them anchored. This likely isn't someone with authority, though, as they are more rebellious than an Eight with a Nine wing, which means they're not usually trusting of authority figures in general.

An Eight with a Nine wing is less likely to be aggressive, unless the situation calls for it. The Nine in them prefers to avoid confrontation, but their Eight certainly doesn't fear it. However, because of the Eight's tendency to lean into conflict and the Nine's tendency to lean away from it, there's an internal tension that could cause an outburst at any moment. It's uncomfortable tension to manage on a daily basis, so you may find them more rigid or stubborn than an Eight with a Seven wing.

That said, they're typically wonderful advocates for social justice, fighting for what's right and being a voice to the voiceless. They are good at seeing different perspectives and leading others with an inspiring confidence. Their unwavering support of those in their inner circle allows others to see them as strong and safe.

Getting Along with a Type Eight

If there is one Enneagram Type that is not **conflict-avoidant**, it's the Eight. They are full steam ahead on confrontation and honesty. This value is often seen as frustrating and difficult, but it's actually refreshing when understood in the right way. Eights are direct and don't mean many of the things people interpret as personal attacks. Their tone can make people believe they are being rude when really they are just being honest. In turn, they appreciate the same sort of treatment.

When you are able to communicate clearly and directly with an Eight, they're ten times more receptive to your message. They deeply appreciate honesty and a clear ask from the person they're communicating with. That compliment sandwich from earlier? Don't need it. They like to deal with things without the "fluff" around what you're asking of them or telling them.

Be confident in what you want to say when aiming to resolve conflict with an Eight. Your feelings are valid and you can tell them that. They respect a bold and clear person, but prepare to get that same type of communication in return because that is their style. Remember, they are jelly beans, so don't use pointed or sharp words, even if the Eight seems aggressive or confrontational. Just be clear, calm, and concise.

An example of a healthy confrontation that the Eight will be receptive to may go like this:

Hey, I'd like to talk about ____. I know you didn't mean ____, but I felt ____. Can we work together on a solution?

Choosing a Career as a Type Eight

When I think of Enneagram Eights in the workplace, I think of people who will unapologetically take charge in a fast-paced environment and get the job done. They are great leaders and have a ton of energy to inspire their team. They have a can-do attitude and solution-oriented skills, so they can often solve a problem at a very fast pace.

When I think of fields they could potentially work in, quite a few come to mind! Whether it's a marketing strategist, politician, director, or business owner, they will be motivated to do a great job if their work is solution-oriented and can be done efficiently. Whether it be in the field of law, the military, or entrepreneurship, they will bring their gifts of assertiveness, independence, and influence to a team, but may "bulldoze" their coworkers thoughts and opinions if not careful. Some careers I wouldn't recommend for Enneagram Eights are a secretary or supporting administrative role, customer service at a call center, or any role that tends to get micromanaged. They won't be as motivated at work if they feel unappreciated or if they feel like their boss or leader is trying to control them. Overall, if you give an Enneagram Eight a challenge, it will be conquered.

Type Eight and Faith

The Enneagram Eight is typically passionate, so their faith may be the same way. Confidently standing their ground, they're able to talk about why they believe what they believe in a way that draws others in. They are usually great at doing research and have a desire for knowledge, so I enjoy learning from an Eight's insights.

On the flip side, if they are too dependent on their own strengths and feel skeptical about faith, they will want to be in charge of their own destiny and may reject the idea of a God who wants a relationship with his creation. No matter what side they're on, they would likely enjoy a debate about religion, as they appreciate someone who stands firm in their beliefs.

The Scripture passage I believe is helpful for an Eight is in 2 Corinthians 12:9–10, which reminds us God's strength is shown when we are weak. This gives us all permission to show up as we are, broken and weak, allowing him to be our strength and protection. What a relief for an Enneagram Eight to know that they don't have to only be the protector, but are welcome to be the protected by God. The truth is God will not betray his children, something the Eight can truly rest in. It may be easier said than done, as Eights can struggle with relinquishing control, but the Lord wants the Enneagram Eight to know their vulnerability is safe with him because he is the Protector of his children.

Type Eight in Love

When it comes to love, an Eight is a protective partner, passionate about what and who they love. They are a challenger who also wants to be challenged, so be aware that you may think you're in an argument and they think you're just having a normal conversation. That distinction is very important when it comes to a romantic relationship. Debating is fun for them, so don't be afraid to bring up a topic you may want to play "opinion ping-pong" about so they feel more connected to you.

Despite the Eight's tough exterior, they often seek a soft

place to land where they feel comfortable opening up and being vulnerable. They have to be able to trust you are strong enough to help them up when they are down, so communicate you can handle that role and aren't afraid to be that person for them. This could look like direct communication without much emotion, providing practical solutions when they ask for help, or simply listening and validating their feelings.

If you are an Eight in a relationship, pay attention to your tendency to communicate with dominance and work to treat your partner as an equal. If you feel strongly about something and your partner does as well, be prepared to compromise. Make sure your significant other feels like you see them and that you are speaking *to* them instead of *at* them. Pay attention to your tone when communicating so it doesn't come off sounding more intense than you intend it to be. And above all, trust your partner enough to lower your guard and speak openly from the heart instead of following your instinct for self-protection.

If you are in a relationship with a type Eight, don't be afraid to challenge them to be the best and healthiest version of themselves. Stay independent by working on your own goals and help hold them accountable for theirs. (They can do the same for you!)

Because they value honesty, be sure to bring that to every conversation, expressing how you feel and what you think. Tell them when they are coming on too strong and give them a minute to cool down when it's clear the situation is escalating. Compromising will be a great tool in your relationship, so set that expectation early on!

Type Eights with Family and Friends

Our shadow side is the side of us that comes out around the people we feel most loved or secure with. With their friends or family, a typically confident Eight will seek reassurance as to whether or not they are needed in their loved one's life. They begin to believe they are only valuable for what they can bring to the relationship, so they start to do things to be seen as indispensable. This can make the Eight become clingy and desperate for validation and intimacy. Boundaries can get blurred and their intensity starts to impede on other's peace.

Eights, pay attention to when you start to feel like you're finding ways for people to need you and remember that you are loved just as you are. You have nothing to prove.

If you have someone in your life that is an Eight, here is how you can love and support them well:

1. Go to a workout class or plan some kind of physical activity with your Eight so you can spend time together and match their energy. They have the most energy out of any Enneagram type and are usually pretty active!
2. Be a safe place for them to be vulnerable. Encourage them to share what they may be going through so they don't feel like they always have to be the "strong one."
3. Mean what you say. Your word is your bond when it comes to communicating with a type Eight, so be confident and don't break a promise to them.
4. Help them tackle their to-do list. Eights appreciate someone who will come alongside them and help them get stuff done, so think about what your Eight may need during this time of their life and help meet that need.
5. If you feel like an Eight in your life is getting bossy or taking over while you're hanging out, let them know. Since they tend to show love by taking charge, they might not even realize they're hurting you! Be honest and direct;

and the faster you tell them what is going on, the sooner you'll find resolution.

Advice for Your Type

I know you're going to think, "Nah, I'm good," when you hear about the challenge I have in mind for you, but I really believe it's worth the risk or I wouldn't suggest it.

Pick a time tomorrow and text someone you love and trust. Ask them how they're doing, and then be vulnerable with them about how you're doing when they ask it in return. Open up with them and tell them how you really are. It might be uncomfortable, but it really helps to build deep and lasting relationships.

I'm going to further challenge you to try this not just tomorrow, but every week. When I suggested this to a group of Eights, many of them replied with, "No thanks!" But I'll say again—it's worth it to deepen your bond with those in your inner circle.

A Letter to an Enneagram Eight

Dear Eight,

Our sweet jelly bean. Don't roll your eyes at me. Yes, I did call you sweet. And I told you what to do. Are you already annoyed?

Your hard exterior doesn't fool me, because I know you're soft on the inside and that you'll do anything for those you love, for the underdog, and for the oppressed. The love you give is BIG and beautiful and wonderful, and friend, it's worth the risk.

You're naturally challenging, naturally engaging, naturally a leader, sure. But when I see you, I see a tenderness that only the chosen get to cherish. Don't be afraid to let that tenderness

> show through. You can't control how people love you, but you
> can welcome them into the fortress you've built around you.
>   You are loved, just as you are. We need your leadership as
> you champion the vision ahead, but we love you for your heart
> of gold. We love you, jelly bean.

Are you a type Eight? Before we move on to the next type, there's one thing I want you to know. You can approach God with complete and total vulnerability, knowing he holds your heart with so much care. You can put down being the protector and rest in being protected. Walk in confidence, dear Eight, that you will not be betrayed by God.

Have you learned something new in this chapter? In the lines below, write down what you don't want to forget about this type and answer the following reflection questions:

In what ways do you embody type Eight? Are your habits more of a healthy Eight or an unhealthy Eight?

_____

_____

In what ways do you differ from type Eight?

_____

_____

Do you know anyone who seems to fit type Eight? How might you encourage them toward healthy Eight habits?

_____

_____

What's something you can take from this chapter and apply to your life?

_____

_____

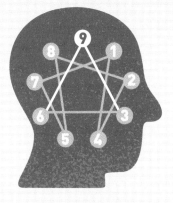

CHAPTER 9

Type Nine:

THE GENTLE PEACEMAKER

You Might Be a Nine If...

1. Confrontation makes you extremely uncomfortable.
2. You put the "pro" in procrastination. You're likely to get lost in smaller tasks and avoid the more important ones that need to get done.
3. You struggle with making decisions. When asked what you want to eat, you usually say, "I don't know, whatever you want."
4. You don't like homework because you want home to be a safe, relaxing place.
5. Nature is usually a calming and soothing place for you.
6. People find you safe and comforting to be around.
7. You're an expert in mediation and seeing both sides of a story.
8. Big social gatherings can be exhausting for you and cause anxiety.

137

9. Even though you are a laid-back person, you know what you believe and will stand your ground.
10. Sometimes you don't want to understand your feelings because you fear what you will find.

Examples of an Enneagram Nine

Blake never seemed to have an opinion about where he wanted to go or what he wanted to do when his group was making plans. He didn't mind what restaurant they went to, which video game they played, or what circuit they focused on at the gym. He was always kind and agreeable, never rocking the boat. Everyone loved him because he was so easy-going and down with what the overall group wanted.

One night during youth group, his small group leader was asking for prayer requests, and when it was Blake's turn to share, tears swelled up in his eyes. Everyone else's eyes widened, wondering what was going on.

He explained he was scared because his dad had been diagnosed with an illness that may not be curable, and they were waiting on some tests. His leader was just as surprised as everyone that Blake was actually sharing something and gave Blake his sympathies. Then he asked, "How long have you known about this?"

Blake said, "A couple of months, but there were a lot of requests, so . . ."

As he trailed off, Blake's leader reminded him, "Every request is important to us. We can handle all of them, and I never want you to put other's needs ahead of your own when you're struggling with something. Thank you for sharing with us, Blake. We are here for you and are praying for your family as you navigate this." Blake instantly felt relief as he saw all the support people gave when he finally spoke up.

Pricelis lives with one of her best friends, BK, whom she loves, but lately she has felt a frustration toward BK that she has never felt before. BK hasn't been pulling her weight when it comes to chores around their dorm room, and Pri has picked up after BK multiple times, hoping she will get the hint. And even though Pri's also huffed and puffed, BK hasn't reacted or cleaned a thing. Pri declined BK's invitations to hang out, which is her way of communicating she's unhappy. She has emotionally withdrawn, and below the surface, anger has been building up.

One day, BK accidentally spilled something on Pri's backpack, and that was *it*.

"UGH! You just can't stay clean, can you?" she exploded.

"Whoa, whoa, what is going on?" BK asked.

"You're not the only one that lives here, you know. It's respectful to clean up after yourself! I can't do it all, and now this? What, do you expect me to clean *this* too?"

The pieces started to fall into place in BK's mind and she replied, "Pri, I had no idea you were upset with me. I wish I could, but I just can't read your mind. If you're frustrated or want me to do something, you have to tell me. I was over here thinking you were organizing and cleaning because you enjoyed it or to procrastinate from studying. I'll work on keeping my stuff cleaner if you can promise to work on communicating with me more."

The anger subsided and tears rose to the brim of Pri's eyes. She promised to work on communication, and they were able to hug it out and go to their favorite ramen place that night.

What Makes Up a Type Nine?

Type Nines are known as the Peacemaker, the Negotiator, the Mediator, or the Accommodator. To know an Enneagram Nine is to truly love an Enneagram Nine. They're warm, inviting, and probably the most supportive friend you have. Their name says it all when it comes to who they are. They are gentle, accommodating individuals who seek internal and external peace with the people and environments around them.

My favorite gift the Enneagram Nine has is the gift of mediation. When presented with an argument, they are truly able to see both sides and where each person is coming from. Because of this, they can help build a bridge of communication between the two parties and guide them to a path of harmony and reunion. I actually sometimes struggle with this when venting to a Nine because I don't always want to see the other perspective, but it always helps in the long run!

Nines struggle with confrontation and conflict, avoiding it at all costs, which may lead to them bottling up their frustrations and finally exploding like Coke when Mentos are added. While they "go with the flow" on the surface, they may actually be seething on the inside, eventually causing them to resent others and withdraw from them.

The thing is, they struggle to show up as the full version of themselves, deciding it's best to suppress their opinions and emotions even though they want to be validated and seen. When they are overlooked or ignored, potentially by bigger personalities or louder people, they can become overwhelmed. When an Enneagram Nine gets overwhelmed, they are likely to drift off into daydreaming or want to lay down to take a nap. This retreating is one of their main avoidance habits. They become what I call a blanket burrito (maybe you remember it from chapter 3), where they just need to roll up in a blanket and watch TV or go to sleep in an effort to escape whatever is stressful or overwhelming to them in the moment.

This is a helpful self-care habit, I'll admit, but when a Nine experiences a prolonged blanket burrito season, it becomes a problem. They'll begin to procrastinate on things they need to do, which can lead to more overwhelm and anxiety. It's helpful for a friend to be there for them to pull them out of a funk. That may look like creating structures and systems for them to simplify everyday tasks and be productive. What can be helpful is someone there to encourage them to do one hard thing each day, whatever that means to them—maybe it's taking time to eat a hot meal, call a friend, or check off something on their list. What's important is that it's a task that can help them regain their confidence and remember their strength.

Their **core fear** is of loss or being separated from those they love, whether that is physically or emotionally. Connection is incredibly important to them, so any threat that it could be broken is very stressful for an Enneagram Nine. One specific fear of theirs is coming across as too needy or divisive and thus pushing people away. In order to avoid this, they default to other people's plans and desires. When you ask them what they want to eat or do, they may reply with, "Whatever you want to do!" While they usually mean it, they are more than likely trying to appease you. It's important to encourage them to use their voice and feel comfortable speaking up if and when they do have a strong opinion or preference.

Whether real or perceived, their **wounding childhood message** is, "Your voice doesn't matter as much as everyone else's" or, "You shouldn't be assertive." Because of this message, they often absorb the energy and emotions of the room or family atmosphere and do everything they can to keep the peace. As you can imagine, this is an exhausting task, so they often retreat to their imagination or daydreams to cope.

Their **core desire** is to have inner stability and a "peace of mind." In order to achieve this, Nines often search for stability in relationships and atmospheres, working to make everyone else happy to create a calm environment. They are also willing to suffer if it means they aren't pushing people away by voicing what they want (even if the pushing away they fear may not actually happen in reality). This can also cause them to hide their feelings if they are upset, because they don't want to upset anyone else. The overwhelm and exhaustion gets too much and then the blanket burrito enters the scene with a side of passive-aggressive communication.

A friend of mine has divorced parents who live in the same city. She is constantly going back and forth from each house, trying to spend equal time with each family so they aren't disappointed. The pressure she and others put on her is exhausting, and she ends up sleeping ten-plus hours at a time because of how tired she is of stretching herself so thin. She desires that peace of mind and inner freedom.

The Different Levels of a Type Nine

The **healthy Nine** knows how important their voice is and is able to confidently share it among their peers, coworkers, or friends. Their confidence is in their identity in Christ, which allows them to fully step into and speak up about who they are, what they think, and how they feel.

While it may be challenging, they understand conflict can be healthy and necessary in some cases to build bridges of communication and trust. One of my favorite things about a healthy Enneagram Nine is that they are able to get involved in a disagreement and bring the peaceful presence a team or group needs. They inspire others with their patience, warmth, and stability as they boldly pursue their calling or purpose in life.

One of my sisters is a Nine and I can immediately tell when she is healthy. She will have a sunny disposition and it's obvious she feels content and confident. Not only that, she starts cracking jokes left and right. I love when I see this side of her!

How do you achieve such a calming influence if you're a Nine? Check out these steps:

1. Show up in the world around you. Don't get caught up in daydreams and fantasies; instead, focus on what is right in front of you. I know this is easier said than done, so try grounding exercises like standing barefoot in the grass and paying attention to all of your senses. What do you hear? See? Taste? Feel? This will allow you to be present and calm any anxiety that may be bubbling under the surface.

2. Remember you are worthy and your presence and needs matter. Speaking up will not push people away; you can invite them in with a refreshing intimacy. If you feel like someone has been distant, talk to them today so you can share the responsibility of reconnecting again—and tell them how you feel. Even if something you did caused the rift, the momentary discomfort of bringing up the issue and hashing it out is worth the long-term benefits.

3. Talk to a counselor or therapist about the root of any anxiety. Ask them to help you take control of reactions like panic attacks or doom thinking, and try exercises like box breathing (see chapter 1 for the steps) or counting to ten and back to zero when those reactions happen. If need be, talk to a doctor as well about the possibility

of medicine that may be helpful for you. While healthy coping mechanisms are enough for some, that may not always be the case and there is no shame in getting help. Talk to your caregivers and your doctor so you all can make the best call for your mental and emotional health.

4. Exercise to release any tension you may be holding on to without realizing it. The reason moving your body is so helpful here is because it's so tempting to just roll up in a blanket and remain sedentary, stewing in your own thoughts. It's important to get your blood moving and get some fresh air as you process anything you may be keeping a tight lid on. The general tension of the world, your unresolved issues in relationships, or anything else that is weighing you down can be a lot to carry. Get moving in your favorite way so you can release what your body is holding inside.

5. Pay attention to passive-aggressive tendencies. When you recognize them, write down how you're feeling and make a plan to address it within yourself and with the person in question. Healthy confrontation is absolutely possible, and it is easier when your thoughts and feelings are organized. Remind yourself that reconciliation is on the other side of that confrontation.

The **average Nine** will do anything to achieve peace within themselves and with those around them. Whether it means burying their true feelings or isolating altogether, they will search for peace at almost any cost. They go along to get along, mirroring those around them and floating along with little direction. If there is someone more assertive near them, they will take on some of their behaviors, attempting to soak up their confidence and find themselves in it. Because of this, it can be challenging to recognize a Nine, as they really show behaviors of each type except for their own! Seeing the world from the viewpoint of others can cause their own to get lost in translation. When confrontation arises, they become anxious and fearful, wanting to just crawl into a hole and hide.

The **unhealthy Nine** doesn't focus on any form of self-care to restore their energy, which leaves them feeling depleted and not starting even the smaller tasks they need to get accomplished. Laziness creeps over them and motivation falls by the wayside. They can also disassociate, which is a feeling of detachment from yourself, people around you, and environment. That is the key marker of an unhealthy Nine, and it can look like addictions or unhealthy habits, as in the numbing, burrito behavior we talked about earlier. I know if I see a Nine in a blanket binge-watching Netflix for days on end, they need support and maybe an outlet for any repressed anger they may be dissociating from.

When under stress, a Nine shows unhealthy attributes of a type Six in how they behave and how they feel. A calm Nine may suddenly become anxious and fearful as their thoughts begin to race, thinking of worst-case scenarios. They may get jumpy and defensive, wondering if something has gone terribly wrong, something they can't think of a solution to because they are unaware of the problem.

If they have been putting things off and avoiding tasks that need to get done, stress will launch them into a hyperactivity of sorts, trying to do it all at once. This causes them to get frustrated with the current pace of the tasks and with their past self for not already taking care of everything. The more stressed a Nine is, the more in denial they are about their needs, which can be difficult on their relationships when those they love are wanting to offer support but don't know how to do so.

Procrastination is a weakness of a Nine, which ends up sending them into a stress tailspin, so if this is you, I recommend pace-scheduling your homework or tasks. Do a little bit every day toward your goal so you don't feel overwhelmed by the task. My mom actually did this with me when I had summer reading in school. I would read one chapter each day so I could complete the books and still enjoy summer with friends. I dreaded starting the reading, but once I finished I was happy I did it!

When in a season of growth, a Nine shows healthy attributes of a type Three in how they behave and how they feel. It's amazing to see an average Nine start to invest in themselves and become a more proactive and self-loving version of who they are.

In growth, they are able to own their voice and stand up for what they believe in, not worrying about judgment or pushback from those around them. They are more assertive and warmer, becoming a magnetic presence. They are able to pace themselves to get their goals completed on time and with joy as their confidence skyrockets!

Many of the Enneagram Nines I know enjoy running, and I've noticed they are more apt to sign up for a race during their season of growth. This is awesome because it gives them a goal and accountability to prepare for that goal in the days between signing up and race day. The more they achieve their smaller goals leading up to the bigger one, the more confident they become in every area of life! The drive and ambition they feel during a season or moment of growth will be shining through them and everyone around them notices.

The **wings** for this type are Eight and One—the Challenger and the Moral Compass. Remember, wings are on either side of your main type and add a little flavor to your personality! A Nine with a One wing is generally more cerebral and principled, focused on fairness and making sure everyone in a situation is okay. Even though a Nine hates confrontation with every fiber of their being, Nines with this One wing are the best mediators, as they are able to see both sides of the issue and reach the most fair and logical conclusion.

This specific type combination is also the best advice giver because they're able to empathize with you while keeping you grounded in the truth of the matter. While they can habitually suppress their own emotions, they are amazing caretakers of the emotions of others. They are thoughtful, kind, and a soft place to land for anyone around them. That said, they often need help from others in remembering to take care of themselves and give themselves grace. This type combination will likely put a lot of pressure on themselves, but they will lead with integrity and honor.

The Nine with an Eight wing is full of tension, as the Eight is easily ignited while the Nine seeks peace—so there is a dollop of stubbornness that naturally happens within them. An internal seesaw, if you will. They are generally easygoing, but if you mess with someone they love, their protective bear comes out instantly! You will see their fire and love for those near and dear to them in a way that may shock you in its intensity. I love this about them because they are gentle yet unafraid to fight for others.

As opposed to the Nine with a One wing, the Nine with an Eight wing is more sociable and engaging, generally with more energy and confidence as the Eight side of them shines through. This combination is like a human version of fire and ice, where their Eight may act up and the Nine has to deal with some repercussions . . . though it's likely the Eight just came out and said or did what was necessary, while the Nine part of them struggles to cope with it.

Getting Along with a Type Nine

When **resolving conflict** with an Enneagram Nine, try to put on your own Nine hat and frame it as anything but conflict. Listen patiently to a Nine and encourage them to really communicate how they are feeling or what they are thinking. Releasing those things is a big deal for them, and they may feel extremely uncomfortable, so offer to be a safe place as you navigate toward a resolution.

Listen well, repeat what you believe you've heard so you're both on the same page, and absolutely bring in the compliment sandwich we already have talked about with other types. Do not pressure the Enneagram Nine to tell you everything in their heart and head at one time. They may need to revisit the conversation once they have sorted it out. Let them know they will not lose you if they really tell you their point of view. It's important to encourage Nines to speak up for themselves. Remind them that you value their opinion and desires.

An example of a healthy confrontation a Nine will be more receptive to may go like this:

Hey, I really appreciate when you did _____ and made _____ impact. It showed you are caring and thoughtful, and I appreciate that. Can we talk more about _____? I'd like to hear you out and share some ideas so we can figure out an easy solution. You are someone I trust, and I hope you feel the same way toward me.

Choosing a Career as a Type Nine

When considering a career for an Enneagram Nine, consider the desire to create harmony and stability within the work environment and the world around them. The more meaningful the work, the more a Nine will feel energized and accomplished in their role. One of my friends is a Nine and she is phenomenal at her job as a school psychiatrist because of the gentle guidance she provides for her students. This is a great career choice for an Enneagram Nine. Social work in general is well suited to a type Nine, as well as philanthropy, family law, and writing! The patience Nines can bring to a classroom is also something worth noting.

A few roles I wouldn't quite recommend for an Enneagram Nine are a referee, politician, or someone in a medical role who deals with high-risk situations. A Nine's natural fear of loss will be heightened in that sort of environment and could take a harsh emotional toll.

Regardless of their job title, as long as the Nine feels heard and can feel supported with a team or one teammate, they will thrive!

Type Nines and Faith

Because of their desire for connection, the Nine is usually one to explore faith and a relationship with God. They are probably the most grounded type in the Enneagram, and faith is one way they are able to achieve such a groundedness.

The closer they are to the Lord, the more they are able to speak up for themselves and their opinions, desires, and dreams. They finally believe their voice matters because they are a child of God. However, when they drift away from the Lord, they may numb out and see other people as more loved or more valued than they are instead of remembering their inherent worth in Christ. When a Nine feels far from the Lord, I encourage them to go on a long walk so they can reconnect with his creation and remember how much he loves them. The Lord is inviting his sweet Nine to adventure with him, hand in hand. He wants the

Enneagram Nine to know that inner peace is found in him, and he wants to provide that for his children so they find true rest in him.

Type Nines in Love

A type Nine brings extreme care and comfort to their partner, always wanting to make them feel supported and seen. They're patient and work hard to create a harmonious environment, both in their surroundings and in their relationships. They will drop everything to be there for their partner if needed and provide unwavering support.

It can be challenging, though, if a Nine feels an argument or tension coming on, because they may disassociate or avoid it to keep the peace. It's important to work things out in relationships, which can be difficult for Nines. If you are working through conflict resolution in your relationship with a Nine, do so in a way that reminds them that everything will be okay and that peace will be restored. The idea that you are on a team will help them feel like you are in it together rather than against each other.

If you are a Nine, be aware of your tendency to repress anger and act in a passive-aggressive way. When you feel these things start to creep in, it's time to vocalize what you are thinking and how you are feeling. Remind yourself you don't have to let go of your inner peace and that there is such a thing as healthy conflict. I know, I know, but I promise it's real!

If you are in a relationship with a type Nine, facilitate some healthy conflict so they really see not all conflict is bad. Remind them you are a team and have a common goal of a strong relationship. Nines tend to thrive when there's structure, so plan weekly date nights that are intentional and dependable. They are highly empathetic people who are more worried about your well-being than their own, so encourage them to take time for self-care.

Lastly, help empower their voice by asking their opinions about topics they care about. They probably don't have a strong opinion about what restaurant you eat at, but they may have some thoughts on what's going on in the world or in their circle of friends.

Type Nines with Family and Friends

When a Nine is with the people they feel the safest with, they may begin to overtly ask for validation of their accomplishments or value as a person. They want to be recognized and noticed, and they can grow tired of wondering where they stand with people. Thus, when they are among those they love, they can be more vocal about their need for reassurance or validation. A typically humble Nine may even start bragging and carrying on about their accomplishments.

If they perceive someone is being critical of them, they may take it harder than you'd expect, but in an effort to hide the emotion, they might create "busy work" for themselves, focusing on things that don't matter instead of facing what they should process. Nines, pay attention to when you start to feel like you're trying to distract yourself from what you really should be focused on.

If you have someone in your life that is a Nine, here is how you can love and support them well:

1. Find a way to spend time together doing something chill. This could be baking, cooking, watching a movie, playing a game—anything that helps the Nine relax and unwind.

A night where you hang out on the couch with some chocolate chip cookies and popcorn is very refreshing to a Nine, and they will love that time together.

2. Gently check in with them when it comes to their emotional or mental state. They don't want to be "too much," so it's not likely they will reach out to initiate a conversation about how they are doing. Be the safe place for them to share what they may be going through.

3. Tell them that their voice and opinion matters! It's a big deal for a Nine to express themselves and their ideas or opinions, so make sure they feel validated when they do. Nines are afraid of being judged, so it's important for them to know you won't judge them, whether it's a confession, a messy car, or music taste!

4. Initiate hang outs. Like I said before, Nines are fearful of being a burden to you or your schedule, so they are less likely to reach out. This can sometimes lead the friendship to be left on the back burner, so try to avoid letting that happen.

5. Never call them lazy. Even if your Nine is becoming apathetic toward things they were previously passionate about, it's not going to change their behavior if they feel shamed or made fun of. Check the steps above for supporting them through this "sloth state."

Advice for Your Type

Nines, I have a little challenge for you. This week, I want you to try things you normally wouldn't do out of fear of judgment. Just try something that has interested you and see what happens.

Give your opinion, even if it isn't asked for, and engage in healthy conversation that may have a dash of confrontation in the mix. This may sound scary, but surviving the temporary discomfort will boost your confidence.

A Letter to an Enneagram Nine

Dear Nine,

Come, curl up next to me on the couch. Here's a cozy blanket, a hot meal from your favorite cookbook, and a warm cup of coffee. Thank you for holding space for me. Can I do the same for you?

You are so good at offering a new perspective. Thank you for always being open-minded and slow to judge. You are a safe place for everyone around you. Know that you can let others be that for you too. You don't have to minimize your heartache to carry ours.

Don't let resentment steal your shine. Tell me what's on your mind and heart. We can have healthy conflict, I promise. You are so loved, kind Nine.

Are you a type Nine? Before we move on, there's one thing I want you to know. Jesus died on a cross for you—remember that when doubt starts to creep in. Remember your voice matters, so raise it accordingly! You are welcome here. Walk in confidence, dear Nine, that you matter to the King of the universe.

Have you learned something new in this chapter? In the lines below, write down what you don't want to forget about this type and answer the following reflection questions:

In what ways do you embody type Nine? Are your habits more of a healthy Nine or an unhealthy Nine?

_____

_____

In what ways do you differ from type Nine?

_____

_____

Do you know anyone who seems to fit type Nine? How might you encourage them toward healthy Nine habits?

_____

_____

What's something you can take from this chapter and apply to your life?

_____

_____

CHAPTER 10

Bonus Chapter:

A FEW MORE LAYERS

If you've ever seen the movie *Matilda*, you may remember one of the most iconic scenes of the early nineties: a giant chocolate cake is placed in front of Bruce, and no one can leave school until he finishes it.

There's more to the story, of course, but when I think about that scene, I think about the Enneagram. It's big and overwhelming at first, but as you get through it little by little, it gets easier and easier. So far, we have covered a lot of ground on our Enneagram journey, but it doesn't end there! If you're ready for more cake, here are a few more layers for you to chew on (and these still don't cover *everything* about the Enneagram!).

Triads: Triads split the Enneagram into three groupings based on something those types have in common. The most popular triad uses the centers of intelligence, where each type is grouped based on whether the people in them usually follow their heart, head, or gut instinct.

Tritypes: These are the types we use as defense mechanisms within the Enneagram, in the order we use them. When under stress, we first deploy our main type's defense mechanism. But if that doesn't work, we then deploy another type's—the one we most identify with from within another triad. If that still doesn't work, we try a different type's defense mechanism from the last remaining triad.

For example: I am a type Two. My tritype is 2–7–8. So when my Two defense mechanism fails me in a situation, I'll deploy the Seven's defense mechanism, and then the Eight's if that doesn't work to achieve my goal.

Subtypes: Each Enneagram type can be split into three subtypes based on which instinct someone uses as a survival method. The three subtypes in each Enneagram type are Self-preservation, Social, and One-to-one.

Now let's break those terms down a little more.

Triads

Imagine you have nine people in a room, and you want to put them into three groups. There are many ways you could divide them, right? If you had three brunettes, three blonds, and three redheads, you could easily divide them that way and we could call that way the "hair triad."

The same can be said about triads within the Enneagram. There are multiple ways to group the types into three, but the most popular triad is the Centers of Intelligence. This triad basically describes how you observe, receive information, and respond to it in life. Beth McCord says it best when she says this about the Centers of Intelligence: "Within this triad, an emotional imbalance, as well as a common desire, drives each Enneagram type. A person will process, react, and respond to life from their Center of Intelligence first."[1]

As you read the information below, it may seem like the types within each triad have nothing in common, much less a common desire! This is because in each triad, one of the types externalizes the emotion, one type internalizes it, and one ignores the emotion, so the behaviors from the different types look very different from each other, even though they're addressing the same emotion.

For example, you may not think a type Seven would struggle with anxiety, but they do because the thought of feeling bored or stuck in a negative emotion can cause this reaction. They just express it by redirecting their energy into something that's fun and exciting! Out of the other two types in the triad, one will usually internalize the emotion they struggle with and the other will externalize it.

So what are the Centers of Intelligence triads? I'm so glad you asked.

The Gut Triad includes types Eight, Nine, and One. All three types struggle with the emotion of anger and the desire to seek justice. They lead and make decisions with their gut instinct. In this grouping, the type Eight externalizes their anger, the Nine tries to ignore it, and the One internalizes it.

The Heart Triad includes types Two, Three, and Four. All three types struggle with the emotion of shame, and all share a desire to have a significant identity. They lead and make decisions based on how they feel about someone or something. In this grouping, the type Two externalizes shame by focusing on the feelings of others, the Three tries to ignore all feelings, especially shame, and the Four internalizes their shame, focusing on how they feel about it as well as other big emotions.

The Head Triad includes types Five, Six, and Seven. All three types struggle with the emotion of anxiety or fear, and their shared common desire is to have security. They lead and make decisions using what they think about someone or something. In this grouping, the type Five internalizes their fear, the Six externalizes it, and the Seven tries to ignore it completely.

If you're having trouble figuring out your enneagram type, look into the triads and see which center of intelligence resonates most with you. That should narrow it down to three options you can begin sorting through. After reading about the triads, do you feel like you resonate with the head, heart, or gut? Your main type is likely within that space.

There are other ways to group the types in various triads, which we'll cover in the next leg in your enneagram journey. To learn more about the different triad possibilities, check out Dr. Drew Moser's book *The Enneagram of Discernment*, or visit Dr. David Daniel's website at dr.daviddaniels.com. They both provide a wealth of knowledge on this topic!

Tritypes

As you read through the Enneagram types, did more than one resonate with you? It happens quite often. People can second-guess their type because they behaviorally bounce between two or three types. Even I second-guess my type every now and then!

In 1995, Katherine Fauvre conducted a study that led to her belief that each person in fact has three types. This is called a tritype. Within your main type, you'll have a specific defense strategy to avoid your core fear and achieve your core desire. When that type's strategy doesn't work, you would then go to the following triad and see which type within that grouping you most identify with, and deploy that type's defense strategy. If that still doesn't work, then you'd move on to the type you identify with from the last remaining triad.

This is a really rich layer of our Enneagram cake, so I'll stop there before we get too full, but if you want to learn more, Fauvre covers this in her book, *The 27 Tritypes Revealed*.

Subtypes

Subtypes are instincts we use as a survival mechanism. There are three different subtypes for each type: Self-Preservation, Social, and One-to-One. While we use all three of them in our lives, each person typically has a primary and secondary subtype, and the third is rarely engaged. If you know someone who has your same Enneagram type but you are incredibly different from one another, the cause may be that you have different subtypes.

To grasp the idea of subtypes, I think of water—it can exist in solid, liquid, or gas form. It's the same matter, but it presents very differently in each way. You may be a certain Enneagram type, but your subtype "form" can mean you seem different than someone else with your type. The key here is that you both, at the core, have the same motivation.

Let's briefly look over each subtype:

People with the **Self-Preservation** subtype are focused on keeping themselves physically and materially safe. Typically, these people are more introverted, and they are focused on preparation and having sufficient food, shelter, and other survival necessities. When they are around others, they may feel like they need to be more aware of their surroundings or supplies, depending on who they are with.

People with the **Social** subtype are focused on their position in a group of people or their connection to power within the group. Their point of view as far as survival goes is that "it takes a village," not just in raising kids but in surviving. They desire to have a positive impact on people and generally are more outgoing and enthusiastic.

People with the **One-to-One** subtype are focused on deep relationships and primarily surviving in a partnership. They are typically more competitive and emotionally intense because they prefer depth instead of surface-level relationships. They're usually assessing each person they encounter to feel out the chemistry and see if there is or isn't a level of compatibility.

Because these three subtypes are within each main type, that means there are twenty-seven instinctual subtypes. Beatrice Chestnut dives further into each in her book *The Complete Enneagram*, but I love to highlight this number because it proves how unique we all are, even if we share a type. I can think of three other people with my same type who seem quite different from me because of our subtypes, wings, or level of health.

What Now?

Have you found your type yet? How did it feel? Were you relieved to know there are other people like you? Or did it make you uncomfortable and want to never open this book again? Ha!

Typically, a person doesn't settle into their main type until their twenties, so give yourself time if you're still figuring it out. The Enneagram can be deep, challenging work to process and go through, especially when we talk about the wounding childhood messages. When you consider the message that resonated the most with you, think about where that may have originated, and if it's too painful to face, reach out to a professional for counseling.

Remember, the Enneagram is just a tool. When I discovered my type, I talked with my counselor about the childhood messages and was able to get a lot of clarity on where they originated, why I was so impacted by them, and what I can do to find healing faster. As I found healing, I was able to show up in the world as a healthier version of myself and operate in my true identity. If you don't feel comfortable seeing someone in person, I recommend an online service like Faithful Counseling. I love being able to speak to someone from the comfort of home.

(Here is a link to find them: faithfulcounseling.com/ainsleyb.) I hope this is a helpful tool, not only when it comes to processing your Enneagram type and everything you just learned, but also the childhood messages associated with it. Counseling is an incredible resource, and I think everyone should try it out if they have the means to do so!

Homework, As If You Don't Have Enough Already

The hike doesn't stop here, my friend. You are well into your Enneagram discovery journey, but there is still so much ahead of you! Here are your next action steps.

Do More Research

This book only covered a few layers of our Enneagram cake, and there is much to more to dig into! I hope you'll continue exploring through other authors, teachers, and resources. Here are a list of my favorites, the resources I personally love and can't study the Enneagram without:

- YourEnneagramCoach.com
- *More Than Your Number* by Beth and Jeff McCord
- TheEnneagramInstitute.com
- *The Road Back to You* by Ian Morgan Cron and Suzanne Stabile
- *The Path Between Us* by Suzanne Stabile
- *The Journey Home* by Meredith Boggs
- *The Journey Toward Wholeness* by Suzanne Stabile (I love her, okay?)
- Anything by Pastor Tyler Zach at GospelforEnneagram.com, but specifically his Enneagram History course.

- Sleeping at Last's album *Atlas* (They created a podcast that explains their whole process of recording each song and all of the details that went into it that I recommend checking out as well. My Enneagram Four friends will really love it. As I write, I'm listening to it as well as the instrumental version!)
- *The Complete Enneagram* by Beatrice Chestnut
- *The 27 Tritypes Revealed* by Katherine Fauvre
- *The Enneagram of Discernment* by Dr. Drew Moser
- DrDavidDaniels.com

I hope this book will be a part of your resource list too as you continue to study more about yourself and your specific type!

Keep the Enneagram in Its Rightful Place

We touched on these points in the beginning, but I want to remind you of some important notes about the Enneagram. Here are some things to remember as you continue on your Enneagram journey:

1. The Enneagram is just a tool to better understand yourself, not an end-all, be-all about you and who you are, or something that determines your destiny. Do not elevate it or rely on it too much.
2. It's a cake, not an onion. The layers build on each other. If you're struggling to understand something, try going back to the previous thing you learned.
3. It should never be used as a sword or a shield. Don't use it to shame, blame, or make excuses when it comes to yourself or others.
4. We are all types in varying degrees, and all the things that go into the subtypes and tritypes, and even your

personal experiences, mean no one person is like
another even within the same main number.

5. True change comes from partnering the Enneagram
with the gospel and finding healing for any childhood
wounds or core fears we may still be struggling with.

6. If you still have trouble finding your type after
researching, seek out a coach to help you sort through
your questions. There are plenty out there ready and
willing to help!

Be More Self-aware

As you consider what type you may be, think about your actions,
the motivators behind them, and how you can approach your
relationships with others in ways that are harmonious and have
boundaries. It's a tricky balance, but I believe in you! The more
you learn about yourself, the more you're able to do that. If you
are interested in some resources for general self-awareness, I'd
love to share a few of my favorites:

- Brené Brown's Netflix special *A Call to Courage*
- *The Gifts of Imperfection* by Brené Brown
- *How to Win Friends and Influence People* by Dale
  Carnegie
- *The Body Keeps the Score* by Bessel van der Kolk
- *Big Magic* by Elizabeth Gilbert

Make a Plan to Adopt Healthier Habits

Whether you use some of the suggestions within the chapters
or choose ones you may have discovered while journaling after
each chapter, don't wait for the new year to start self-improving!
Start by trying just one or two small changes and gradually
build from there.

Be more empathetic to those around you. This won't be challenging for some types, but for others, this is a huge step toward growth. It's not always easy to commit to taking time to understand someone else's point of view, but it'll be worth it when you see your relationships grow and flourish!

Put boundaries in place. Again, some types are traditionally great at this while some struggle, but setting healthy boundaries is an important skill for all types to master. It's been life-changing for me, and I believe it will be for you too if you feel like you are spread too thin or like you're being taken advantage of.

Make time for consistent self check-ins to see where you're at. Celebrate your wins, and be honest with yourself if there's something you need to change or work on. I'm hopeful our time together has brought some self-awareness, enlightenment, and confidence to who you are and why God made you the perfect way he did.

Since one of my favorite ways to process and self-reflect is journaling, I thought I'd provide some journal prompts for each Enneagram type. Grab a notebook and think through the questions for your type, using them as a springboard as you continue learning and growing.

1. What does being "good" mean to you? Are you putting too much pressure on yourself as you work toward this ideal? How can you give yourself grace while maintaining your moral standard?

2. Are you overextending yourself, bending boundaries, and feeling taken advantage of? Who do you feel like you'd be disappointing? If it's not yourself, then it's probably time to put a boundary in place. What boundaries will you set moving forward, and how will you enforce them?

3. Are you molding your image to fit someone else's idea of success? Take some time to think about who you are and the gifts that only you hold. What are you keeping in your life solely because it's impressive to others? Is it time to let it go?

4. Are you letting your emotions win most of the time? How can you ground yourself so you feel in control of them instead of vice versa? What can you do for others to refocus your attention on someone else?

5. Are you resisting a feeling you'd rather not face right now? What would it look like to process it, even for only fifteen minutes? How can you focus on being present instead of avoidant?

6. Are you worried about the "what ifs" and "what abouts"? Take some time to remember you can trust your own instinct and be strong in a decision. What else can you do to build your self-confidence? Who can you reach out to for support?

7. Are you chronically chasing after the next best thing? Are you fantasizing about what excitement it may hold? Take some time to be present where you are and appreciate the place you are in. Instead of planning the next adventure, how can you settle into the here and now?

8. Are you guarding yourself against someone or something right now? What is it and why? Can you think of a safe person you're able to be vulnerable with? What would it look like if you texted them and asked for help?

9. Are you avoiding doing something because you fear judgment or because you're trying to please others? Try not to let other people's perceptions steal your joy and dictate your actions. Will you make a list of things you love about yourself and operate in that confidence as you make decisions moving forward?

You can revisit these journal prompts every month as an internal check in. You can even ask a friend these questions or do these journal prompts together—it's a great way to connect with them to see how they are feeling and how they are growing. My prayer is that you will feel more equipped each month to tackle any challenges you're facing head-on!

Pop Quiz Revisit

Remember that pop quiz from the introduction? Or did you just read that and immediately flip here to check if the answers were in the back? Either way, I got you:

Question 1: What is the Enneagram?
Answer: *According to Beth and Jeff McCord, it's a GPS to help you know where you are, where you're heading, and how to get to your healthiest destination. It truly helps us understand the "why" behind some of our thoughts and behaviors.*

Question 2: Is it one of many helpful tools or the only one we should ever use?
Answer: *It's one of many helpful tools.*

Question 3: Fill in the blanks: The Enneagram should never be used to _____ or _____ anyone.
Answer: *shame or blame*

Question 4: The Enneagram is helpful information, but where is transformation found?
Answer: *Transformation is found in the Lord.*

Homework and a quiz? Yikes. Let's take a commercial break with some fun Enneagram facts, shall we?

Fun Facts

Have you ever wondered what your favorite celebrity's Enneagram type is? I have!

Admittedly, I haven't spoken to anyone on the list below to confirm their types, but here are a few ideas!

- Famous type Ones: Michelle Obama, Celine Dion, Captain "Sully" Sullenberger, Joan of Arc
- Famous type Twos: Pope John XXIII, Dolly Parton, Princess Diana, Saint Mother Teresa
- Famous type Threes: Taylor Swift, Tom Cruise, Tony Robbins, Michael Jordan
- Famous type Fours: Alanis Morrisette, Johnny Depp, Vincent van Gogh, Thomas Merton, Dolly Parton(?)
- Famous type Fives: Stephen Hawking, Bill Gates, Jane Goodall, Tim Burton
- Famous type Sixes: Ellen DeGeneres, Mark Twain, Robert F. Kennedy, Eminem
- Famous type Sevens: Robin Williams, Mozart, Amelia Earhart, Paris Hilton
- Famous type Eights: Martin Luther King Jr, Muhammed Ali, Ernest Hemingway, Matt Damon
- Famous type Nines: George W. Bush, Zooey Deschanel, Morgan Freeman, Walt Disney

Ah, that's better. Were there any in that list that surprised you? What type do you think your favorite celebrity is? Celebrity types are actually something I'm often asked about. Once I went on a podcast and they asked me to type the Disney princesses, ha! Here are some of the other most common questions I get asked about the Enneagram.

FAQs About the Enneagram

Which two types are best in a romantic relationship?

This is the question I am asked probably once per week, and I'll tell you this: The beautiful thing about the Enneagram is that each type combination brings different things to the table and creates an interesting dynamic. So there truly aren't two specific types that go best together; what's really important is the health of each person. Two *healthy* types go best together. When you are healthy, you're typically more open-minded and able to clearly communicate what you need from the other person and vice versa. Healthy people are better able to support both themselves and their partners. So if you want to be a good partner, work toward achieving a higher level of personal health.

What about the origins of the Enneagram?

The origins of the Enneagram are complex because so many teachers and thought leaders have taught the Enneagram through the lens of their own worldview, including me! For example, Jeff and Beth McCord say that, "In our presentation of the Enneagram, we have removed or redefined all aspects that do not align with a Biblical worldview. We direct people to spiritual disciplines, not unbiblical spiritual practices. As laid out in our mission statement, our goal seeks to focus people's attention upon the person and work of Jesus Christ."[1] I love this about their company, because I also teach the Enneagram through a Christian worldview and believe that it's useless without the gospel.

The truth is, the Enneagram isn't incredibly clear on its origin and history because there isn't just one source. Nor is it scientifically backed. Yet, when I read about my own type and when I hear other people discover theirs, it's "scary accurate." That's the phrase I hear almost every time. I like it!

If you have questions about the Enneagram's foundation, I highly recommend watching the deep dive study Pastor Tyler Zach did on the origins of the Enneagram, where he debunks and explains some commonly believed myths. It's incredibly helpful and clear when it comes to some general issues people bring up. The video can be found on YouTube by typing in "Gospel for Enneagram Should Christians Use the Enneagram | Dealing with Common Objections." He also has an online course all about the history of the Enneagram if you want to go even deeper. That can be found at tylerzach .com/history.

Does everyone have a wing?

Yes, everyone has both wings, but they choose how much or how little of each wing they want to use. I'll use a personal example. I'm a type Two, which means I have a One wing and a Three wing. If I need to get organized and stay on top of a schedule, for example, I tap into the gifts of my One wing to strategize and get it done. But then if I'm part of a group that needs a leader in a situation, I could use the gifts of my Three wing to step up and provide that leadership, even though I don't always care to be the leader.

Does your Enneagram type change?

Nope! Your Enneagram type, once properly determined, is the same no matter what because it's based on a core desire instead of your personality traits, which change with age, season, and emotion. As I have personally gotten older, I feel like many of my behaviors have changed, but at the end of the day, I'm still 100 percent driven by my core desire.

If I know my Myers-Briggs type, can I determine my Enneagram type?

Different Enneagram coaches or teachers may have different opinions about this specific question, but I personally don't think so. I can assume that if you are an Extrovert, you're less likely to be a type Five, but that's not guaranteed. Plus, your Myers-Briggs type can change as you age or experience life while your Enneagram doesn't change, so it's not necessarily a good indicator of what type you are.

How does someone become an Enneagram coach?

When I tell you that it's one of the best things I have done for myself, I'm not lying! I absolutely love being a coach and I believe if it's something you feel drawn to, it's absolutely worth exploring once you're ready! There is not one type that would be a better coach than another type because everyone brings something different to coaching that is so beneficial, so I'd encourage you to go for it! If you'd like to learn more about the program I used, I have a referral link on my website that can be found at EnneagramWithAB.com.

Is there a way to use my Enneagram to determine what specific career might be best for me?

Truthfully, any type can thrive in any career, but there are some general strengths of each type that can lend themselves better to a certain job. For example, an Enneagram Five is generally more detail-oriented, while a Two is more relational. That means while each is capable of doing jobs that have a focus in either of those areas, it's more about what they would enjoy and thrive in. As long as their core motivation is being fed, they will be just fine doing whatever is asked of them! The more you understand your core motivation, the more clarity you will have. If you have only read your type before landing here, we unpack each type as it relates to a potential career so give each section a read!

How can I manage my "shadow side"?

To avoid giving in to the shadow side, I'd suggest reminding yourself, "The people who love me the most deserve the best of me." This is what I personally practice, and I find it extremely helpful. In addition to this, be sure to take responsibility for unhealthy behaviors when they do happen and apologize. Recognizing and owning the situation will go far with those you love.

What is your favorite Enneagram type?

You'd be surprised at how often people ask me this question! It comes up at the end of almost all of my group sessions. And while I know I'm not supposed to have a favorite, I actually have two. It's a tie between a type Four and a type Eight. Many are surprised by the Eight, but I have found that communication with them is refreshing because they value honesty. I've also found that their inclination to protect their friends and loved ones makes them great secret keepers. Fours are in my top favorites because I feel like I never stop learning with them and they are the most complex type, which keeps me on my toes when I'm guiding people in a session!

Is this a me thing or my type thing?

This is also one of my most-asked questions! Many people wonder if some of their behaviors are because of their type or just because of who they are in general. Of course, I'd need to know what behavior they are asking about in order to answer this question, but a few examples I have addressed with people are:

- An Eight who always wants to be the one to drive: likely a type thing because of their desire to be in control.
- A Two who often feels responsible for the emotions or well-being of someone else: this is a type thing.
- A Five who only watches anime: this is a them thing. That doesn't mean some Fives couldn't share this trait, but it's not an Enneagram-specific detail about their personality.
- In a similar vein, Enneagram Sixes are often true crime junkies, because it can help them feel better equipped in case they are ever in a similar situation. While a love of true crime isn't specific to an Enneagram Six, I have found this preference to be a popular commonality, so this one is actually a mix of their type and their personality.

Well, friend, as we come to an end of our time together (I know, I'm sad about it too), I want to remind you that the Enneagram is just a tool and that you are, indeed, more than just your type. You can use this to help propel you toward your dreams and goals in life, but don't give it too much importance. You're more than a number on the Enneagram, more than your strengths, weaknesses, motivations, and unhealthy attributes. You are an amazing, complex, dynamic, miraculous creation of God, and I'm your biggest cheerleader as you step into a self-awareness that can equip you for a slightly easier journey through life. As you continue on this hike, backpack on and shoes laced, I hope you'll explore new paths, pick up new tools, and meet some amazing people along the way.

A few years ago, my husband and I were hiking an eight-mile, mostly uphill trail in the Pacific Northwest when we met some of the most interesting people. You can create a short-lived but deeply felt bond when you get encouragement from those descending as you ask them, "Is it much farther? Is it worth it?" Every time I asked that question, the person said, "It's absolutely worth it. You can do it!" They could answer with confidence because they'd been there.

So as you wander through your Enneagram journey to discover more about who you are, it may be hard. You may have to face some things you'd rather keep hidden. You may learn things about yourself that feel uncomfortable. But as someone who has done the work and trekked the path before you, I'm here to tell you: It's absolutely worth it. You can do it!

ACKNOWLEDGMENTS

It truly takes a village to raise a child and write a book, so I'd love to thank some of my village who have encouraged and worked with me along the way. The Zondervan team has been so fun to work with. Thank you, Katherine Easter and Jacque Alberta! Every time an email with either of your names pops up, I get excited! Thank you to my literary agent, Trinity McFadden, for responding to my "talk me off the ledge" emails when I thought I wouldn't meet an expectation or deadline.

To my husband, Justin, and daughter, Goldie, for putting up with my hours at the computer—thank you! To Jaymi; you already know I couldn't do this without you!

Thank you to my many friends and family members who let me bounce ideas off of them about their enneagram type and listened to me talk about it at every hangout, party, or dinner. To Meredith Boggs and Tyler Zach, thank you for being my enneagram coach besties! Bethny, Pri, Cass, and Mariela, thank you for your steadfast friendship and for being the best "coworkers." Last but not least, my "chicken nuggets," who constantly inspire me to learn more about myself and stay close to the Lord. LOVE Y'ALL!

NOTES

Introduction

1. Beth and Jeff McCord, *Become an Enneagram Coach Workbook,* Your Enneagram Coach, 2019, accessed via PDF download from The Become an Enneagram Coach program training materials.
2. Ian Morgan Cron and Suzanne Stabile, *The Road Back to You: An Enneagram Journey to Self-Discovery* (Downers Grove, IL: Intervarsity Press, 2016), page 39.
3. *Become an Enneagram Coach Workbook,* Your Enneagram Coach, 2019.
4. *The Road Back to You,* page 39.

Chapter 10

1. *Become an Enneagram Coach Workbook,* Your Enneagram Coach, 2019.

Conclusion

1. Beth and Jeff McCord. "Should Christians Use the Enneagram?" http://yourenneagramcoach.com/origins, accessed May 30, 2023.

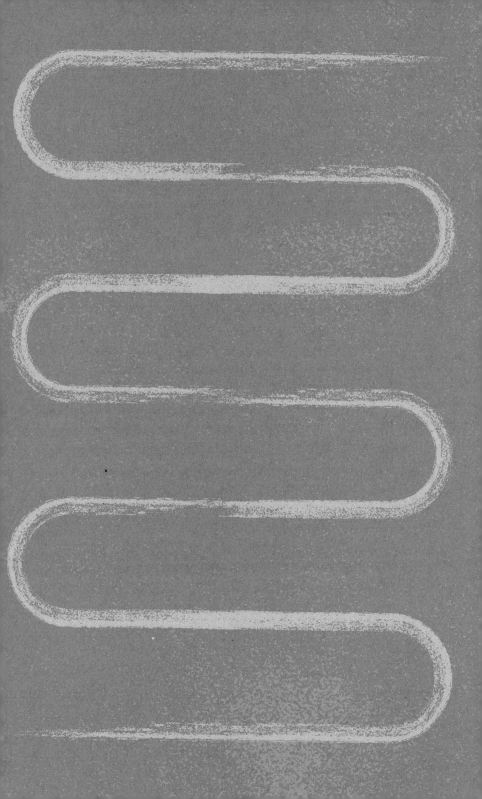

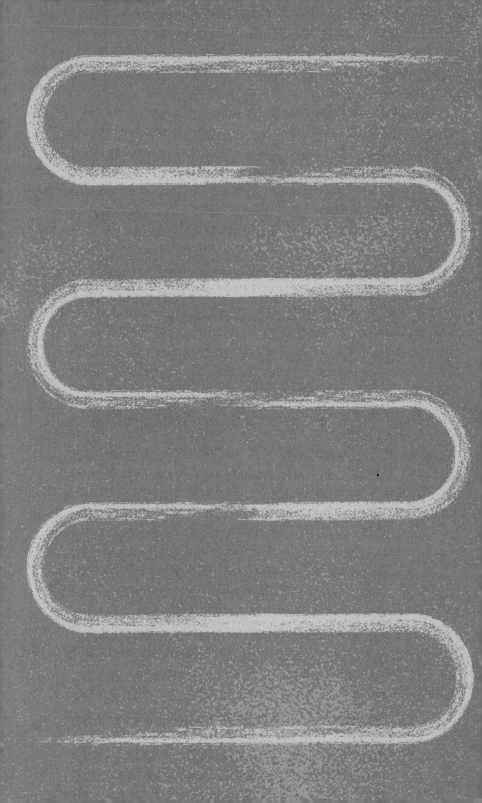